Step Out of the
BOAT

⚓

God Is Waiting to Do Miracles Through You!

LEVI LAND

DESTINY IMAGE™ EUROPE srl
Via Maiella, 1
66020 San Giovanni Teatino (Ch) - Italy

"Changing the world, one book at a time."

This book and all other Destiny Image™ Europe books are available at Christian bookstores and distributors worldwide.

To order products, or for any other correspondence, please contact:

DESTINY IMAGE™ EUROPE srl
Via Acquacorrente, 6
65123 - Pescara - Italy
Tel. +39 085 4716623 - Fax: +39 085 9431270
E-mail: info@eurodestinyimage.com

Or reach us on the Internet: **www.eurodestinyimage.com**

ISBN: 978-88-89127-60-5

For Worldwide Distribution, Printed in the U.S.A.

1 2 3 4 5 6 7 8 / 11 10 09 08

DEDICATION

This book is dedicated to You, Lord Jesus.

You have created us in Your image and likeness. We have sinned, but still You love us. Indeed, You came to this earth to give Your life as a sacrifice for our sin. We are eternally grateful for the enormous magnitude of Your suffering for us, that we might have eternal life, and that we might become joint-heirs together with You. You are awesome, Lord!

I dedicate this book to You and no other one, because You alone are the One who has done the many signs and wonders recorded in this book. You have fulfilled Your promises, helping us to understand that miracles did not cease with the Book of Acts. Rather, we now understand that it was our faith that had ceased. Forgive us for that.

Let Your name be glorified in all You do through Your servants. May every reader see You, Lord Jesus, and You alone.

Thank You, Lord, for Lily, my faithful wife and companion for so many years, for her willingness to also "step out of the boat" and keep her eyes fixed on You through many difficult times, and for her amazing love and arduous labors in raising our large family. For such enormous blessings the praise and glory must go to You!

At this time, we both not only dedicate this book to You, but also our lives once again, so that You will strengthen us like the eagles, and we can continue to go forth to the nations, taking Your glorious message to those who do not yet know how much You love them, to those who need healing in their bodies and deliverance from the powers of darkness in their souls.

Lord, let this book speak to many hearts. Your Spirit says to us that, indeed, "The harvest truly is plenteous, but the labourers are few" (Matt. 9:37b). So, Lord Jesus, send forth laborers who will do the things that You did. Our heart's desire is to be with You soon, to love and adore You forever! "Even so, come, Lord Jesus" (Rev. 22:20b).

ACKNOWLEDGMENTS

We want to take this moment to thank our sister in Christ, Vera W., for her loving and willing hands, typing this manuscript at 81 years of age. She and her husband, Don (now with Christ in glory), have been pillars of encouragement to us for many years, and their lives have added countless blessings to ours. Their daughter Dianne (Deedi) assisted in the preparation of this manuscript and continues to help by maintaining computer records and updating our mailing lists.

Also, we thank our dear sister in Christ, Hanna W., for her part in "holding the ropes for us" on the home front and forwarding incoming funds to us, to use in His service as we travel and work in many different places. We are very grateful to each of them and to many of you who have given whatever you can in order that the Gospel be proclaimed over these last four decades. We have no desire to retire, for the joy of serving Him is our strength.

Most of all, thanks to our Lord Jesus Christ, who for the joy that was set before Him endured the cross, that we might become joint-heirs together with Him (see Heb. 12:2; Rom. 8:17). May He add to each of us daily, a bigger portion of His love as we reach out to souls in need around this globe.

TABLE OF CONTENTS

PREFACE

- Are miracles still happening today?
- Does God still heal the sick, cause the blind to see, and the deaf to hear?
- Are the miracles you read about in the four Gospels and the Book of Acts still occurring now?

I trust that the testimonies in this book will help you to discover that Jesus truly is the "same yesterday, and to day, and for ever" (Heb. 13:8), that He is fulfilling His promise to perform signs and wonders through those who believe Him, and He is reaching out to those who are ready to come to Him, especially when they see the miracles of our Lord through us.

As simple servants of the Lord, it has taken a while for me, as well as for my wife, Lily, to begin trusting our Father as we ought. Even so, we must share our mistakes and outcomes, believing that they might be of help along your way. As you read this book, hopefully you will understand why we have changed our names and many of the names in the testimonies given; the risk is great for many believers in places where religious freedom is either forbidden or limited. It is our prayer that many of you will also be moved to help bring in the great harvest of souls that is now taking place all over the world, for the time is short, and we love the very thought of His appearing for us in the clouds above.

When you read these testimonies of God's power over sickness and satan, please turn your eyes to Jesus, the author and finisher of our faith. There are many wonderful things that He likewise wants to do through you. His name is wonderful. Let His wonders fill your heart and His praise be continually on your lips. Look not back, neither to the right, nor to the left. Look upward to Jesus, into His loving face, and praise His holy name. "Bless the Lord, O my soul: and all that is within me, bless His holy name" (Ps. 103:1). May these testimonies help you to lift your eyes to Jesus, for if you will say, "Lord, if that is You, bid me to come unto You," He will indeed say, "Come" (see Matt. 14:28-29).

Let not your heart be troubled, neither let it be afraid. Though we fail, His hand is there to pull us up as well as to correct our errors. He has been waiting for this moment, and so have you. Step out of the boat of natural security; then every obstacle, every adversity, every doubt and fear will be overcome, as you keep your eyes focused on Him!

We have a precious Savior and Lord who fulfills all His promises. We pray that you will see only Him, who alone is worthy of all the glory and honor. May our heavenly Father make this book a source of many blessings to you. Thank you for holding us in your prayers.

Brother Levi and Sister Lily

Chapter One

A Crazy Man Set Free

⚓

It was in a little town in Chiapas, southern Mexico. A group of about 50 pastors from the surrounding villages had gathered in a quaint church on a hilltop to learn more from the Word of God. No one had ever attended Bible school or seminary, but all ached with a deep hunger for the things of God, and a love for the people.

As I opened the Word to the pastors that first morning, I glanced across the group and noticed one lady sitting amongst them, whose eyes were filled with a deep spiritual hunger. At the end of that first meeting, she approached me with a pleasant, but worried expression.

"My name is Maria," she said. "I am told that you might help me."

I listened as Maria explained her problem.

"I have two sons," she continued. "One is a successful veterinarian here in this town. The other, Armando, the younger, has a severe mental problem, and several times has tried to kill me."

I could not imagine why any son would want to do harm to this very sweet mother. With tears welling up, Maria attempted to maintain a courageous front as she went on.

"Armando wanted his own cattle ranch, so I bought him a 500-acre ranch not far from here. But still he was not happy. When he was a child, his father had often treated him with rejection, and this has made him both sad and angry.

"Recently, I decided to take him to a psychiatrist in Mexico City. The trip was planned under the guise of another purpose; otherwise, he would not have gone. Unfortunately, that visit to the psychiatrist infuriated Armando, and he came out of the office saying, 'He's the one that's crazy, not me!' Since that day, he has been very unpredictable, and has tried on occasion to kill me. There is something diabolical inside of him. I can see it in his eyes," she choked, finally breaking down in tears.

"I am sorry," I consoled her, and then I offered "How can I help you?"

"Can you find time to go and pray for my son? I would be so grateful."

I assured Maria that I would, and we agreed on eight the next morning, a Tuesday. She would pick me up in her car and drive me to her son Armando's ranch, which was only 30 minutes away.

The next day, as we traveled on winding roads amongst the hills of a beautiful part of the country, there was promise of good weather, but within, I was feeling a bit apprehensive. Yet as we reached the gate of Armando's ranch, the Holy Spirit gave me assurance of His presence. (And I was going to need it.)

As we came to a stop, I noticed that Armando was rushing out of the house to open the gate. We then pulled in, and I got out. As I circled around the car, I was stunned to see Armando pulling out a machete from behind him. Raising it over his mother's head, he shouted, "Now, get ready to die! This is your end!"

There was only one recourse—the name of Jesus!

"Put down that machete, in the name of Jesus!" I shouted. He complied. But the more he talked, the more furious he became, and again, the machete was raised over Maria's head!

"Put that machete down, in the name of Jesus!" I commanded once again. And again, he lowered it.

Lord, help me! At a loss of what to do next, I prayed within. Suddenly it occurred to me to ask him a question.

"Armando, what a beautiful ranch you have! Do you have a river on it?"

"Yes, it is down there. Go take a look at it," he insisted.

"Well, not right now. I'll rest up first," I answered.

Not caring for my response, he continued. "Go see the river!" Not wanting to argue, I went to see the river, while interceding in my heart for the life of his mother.

As I walked toward the water, I perceived Armando's shadow as he followed behind me, machete in hand; and at one point, I turned slightly to see his mother nervously sweeping the porch and walks. A few minutes later, we arrived at the river, and I commented to Armando how beautiful it was, even though inwardly, I was not really enjoying it at all. Then I sat down on a rock.

"Take off your shoes, and put your feet in the water," he commanded.

"The water is very cold for that, just now. Maybe in a few hours the sun will warm it up," I muttered.

"Take off your shoes!" again he ordered. "And put your feet in the water!"

I could not argue with a machete, and so I did as he said. Armando then quickly snatched up my shoes and walked a distance to hide them behind a bush.

Upon returning, he announced, "Now, let's walk down river." This was not an easy task, because my bare feet were not used to walking on river stones. Nevertheless, I continued to walk and talk.

"Armando, what beautiful cattle!" I commented. "Are they yours?"

"Yes," he replied briefly. "And you see that hammock, between the trees up on the hill? I made it, and I want you to try it out."

As we walked up the hill toward the hammock, I began to suspect Armando's motives.

"Get in it," he ordered.

"Well, Armando, you see, it's not quite my siesta time," I choked, trying to think of a reason to avoid the hammock.

"I said, get in it!" he shouted.

As I obeyed his orders, my prayers were fast ascending from within. But for some reason, I did not feel the need to command that the machete be put away in Jesus' name. Suddenly, he raised the weapon over my head, and as he was preparing to decapitate me, he shouted, "Okay, you psychiatrist, now you die!"

"Whoa!" I gasped. "Hold everything! I am not a psychiatrist!"

"Then, who are you?" he roared.

"I am Brother Levi," I replied, just barely able to get it out.

Then he lowered his machete. "And how do I know you are not a psychiatrist? Let me check your pockets to see if you have any pills."

Interestingly, that morning, I had meant to put some aspirins in my pocket for a toothache, but had forgotten to do so! He turned my pockets inside out and found no pills.

"So why did you come here?" he pried.

"Because I want to be your friend," I answered.

"My friend? My best friend died last week."

"Really? What was his name?" I asked.

"Pancho," he said sadly. "He was my dog. He's buried right over there. Come, I'll show you his grave."

We arrived at Pancho's grave where the flowers were now wilted. I sensed that it was important to Armando that I spend a few moments in silence and respect for the memory of his best friend.

"I should cry, but I can't," he lamented.

I then looked at my watch. "Armando, I hate to leave, but I must because I have a meeting this afternoon. Can you take me to my shoes?" I wondered how he would react.

"Let's go," he replied.

As we walked back up along the river, I prayed, asking God for wisdom, and for Armando's willingness to be delivered of these spirits of hate and resentment that were controlling him. My heart felt very heavy for this young man, for even his countenance was disfigured by his inner bitterness. *Lord, help me,* I cried as I walked. *Although this man is a victim of satan, surely You have called him to be Your child. I must have Your help, Lord. Fill me with Your Spirit and Your love.*

As we reached the place where we had first come to the river, I sat on a rock while Armando searched the bushes for my shoes. Ten minutes later, he was still searching because he had forgotten exactly which bush he had hidden them under. I thought about how I would look, preaching barefoot for the afternoon meetings. *Maybe God wants more humility in my life,* I wondered. Finally, Armando appeared with my shoes.

As we began to walk back to the house, I could see his countenance changing and the spirit of hate rising up again. I could also see his mother from a distance still nervously sweeping everything that could be swept. I'm sure the sight of Armando carrying his machete, along with his facial expressions and his harsh words did not paint a pretty picture.

"Madre!" He shouted, as we got closer. "Why did you take me to that psychiatrist? He's the one that's crazy, not me!" And with that, he stabbed the machete into the ground.

Lord, I pleaded from within, *I have come here to help this young man, and have accomplished nothing. It is almost time to go, and I don't know what to do. Speak to my heart. How can I help him?* Immediately I felt a peace, and the words that the Holy Spirit spoke to me were clear. *Tell Armando that you must leave now, and as you do, walk toward him, and give him a hug. Then I will show you what to do next.* This was not the answer that I had expected, nor was it the one I wanted. *Lord, please don't ask me to do that! This boy hasn't bathed in weeks, and his odor will stick to my clothing. And then I will stink at the meeting today! There must be another solution.* I was surprised at His answer: *I washed stinky feet. If you cannot do what I ask, do not expect My presence at the meetings.* Instantly, I surrendered. *Lord, You win,* I replied. *But please, hold my nose for me!*

As I moved toward Armando, I said, "Well, Son, I must be going now." And as I reached out my arms to give him a hug, he stepped forward into mine, and embraced me tightly, not wanting to let go. The Lord whispered gently to me, *Hold still there! Be patient! Let Me work in him; I will do it through you!*

Soon, Armando was shaking in my arms, and his tears were falling on my shoulder. My heart was led to pray aloud, "Father, You have called a son unto Yourself. Hold him close!" With these words, Armando began to cough…and cough…and cough…expelling the evil spirits. Again, the Lord whispered, *Don't let go. I am cleaning him out.* In Armando's ear, I spoke, "In Jesus' name, I command all spirits of satan out of Armando. Spirits of hate, vengeance, bitterness, sadness, rejection—you all must go, in Jesus' name!" The coughing continued, and Armando would not release the embrace.

I glanced over to where his mother was watching with tears. She seemed to understand what was happening.

"Armando, our heavenly Father loves you," I told him. "He wants to be your Father, too. He gave His only Son, Jesus, to die for you. Will you open your heart to Jesus, and let Him come in, forgive all your sins, and be your Savior?"

As I spoke, he stopped coughing, and then upon receiving our Savior, he openly forgave all those whom he hated, including the psychiatrist. The next minute he turned and rushed into his mother's arms, asking her for forgiveness with tears. It was a long embrace, and even though I knew that we were running out of time, I understood they could not be interrupted. It was an eternal moment for both of them, but still more, it was a time of rejoicing in Heaven, with the Father and the Son, and the angels. And for me— it was another chapter in my school of faith, a precious experience that will never be forgotten.

As we walked toward the car, I turned to say good-bye to Armando. His face glowed with a big smile, the first I had seen. And the machete? He had forgotten where he had left it. As we drove out the gate, Armando closed it behind us, and with that big smile, continued waving with his hand.

After going a short way down the road, Maria stopped the car. "Will you please drive? I can barely see," she said. Her eyes were filled with tears of joy.

A while later, back in town, I stopped in front of the little church. But before getting out, Maria pleaded, "Please wait. I, too, want Jesus to be my Savior. Will you pray for me?"

What a joyful occasion it became, both in Heaven and on earth! Though very tired from the day's activities, I felt the joy of the Lord renewing my strength as I began teaching the Word that afternoon. The presence of the Lord was very real and sweet to all of us in each of the meetings that followed. After Armando and his mother became new creations in Christ, Armando's brother, Carlos, the veterinarian, was the next to give his heart to the Lord.

For me, it was another important experience in learning to obey our heavenly Father, one step at a time. "O the depth of the riches both of the wisdom and knowledge of God! how unsearchable are His judgments, and His ways past finding out!" (Rom. 11:33).

Our prayer is that Maria and her sons, Armando and Carlos, will not only walk in the ways of righteousness, but that their lives will be multiplied into hundreds more for the glory of our Lord Jesus.

Chapter Two

A VALUABLE EXPERIENCE
IN AFRICA

⚓

As you continue to read of the miraculous events throughout this book, I pray that you will be blessed from above. The names within these testimonies have been changed for two reasons. First, you will understand as you read, that it is necessary for the protection of God's children in many places where there is no longer freedom of worship as we know. For this same reason, I'm using a fictional surname for myself and my wife Lily. Second, we want your eyes to look upon our loving Savior, Jesus, the author and finisher of our faith. He alone is worthy of the praise for the things He does. The apostle Paul says, "To live is Christ" (Phil. 1:21a). To live is neither Levi nor Lily; but to live is Christ, and Him alone. It is He who walks in our shoes, talks through our mouths, heals with our hands, and loves with our hearts. It is He, and He alone, who must receive the glory for the miraculous things that He is doing on earth today, through His children.

I trust that if you believe that signs and wonders are not for today, or if you have thought that the gifts of the Spirit are no longer in use, that you will let the Holy Spirit speak to you in the following pages. It is our prayer that many eyes will be opened as to what our mission is today as children of God. Let me share with you a difficult but valuable experience.

Many years ago, while ministering to a certain tribe in Africa, and still firmly believing in the Cessation Theology (the doctrine that the gifts have ceased), which I had learned in Bible school, I was teaching a small group of new believers in Christ. I had not yet taught on the Great Commission, but they had already read it. Then one day, to my surprise, as I glanced out my window, I saw two of my students coming toward my house, bringing a man with long hair and fetishes hanging around his neck, obviously a witch doctor. Within me, I felt certain that they would ask me to cast out his demons, which I had never done before. Seconds later, there was a temptation to ignore the knock at the door. I didn't know what to do or how to answer them; nevertheless, the Holy Spirit quietly spoke and told me to open the door and follow His instructions. As I did so, both boys spoke at the same time.

"Brother Levi, we brought you this witch doctor."

"I can see that," I remarked, as I wondered what to do next.

"Well, we preached Christ to him, but he did not want to hear it. Instead, he sat on the ground and plugged his ears with his fingers," they explained.

"So, what did you do next?" I asked.

"Well, we thought and thought, and then we remembered what Jesus did, so we decided that was the only thing to do," they answered.

"What is that?" I asked.

"Well, we said, 'Okay, devil, now we know it's you. You get out of this man in the name of Jesus! You've got to go right now!'" they excitedly told me.

"And did the demons go?" I ventured.

"Yes, but first they fought and rolled him all over the ground and made him foam at the mouth. So, well, then we sang a hymn of praise to Jesus. Then they left very fast!"

I stood there nearly in disbelief. *Could this actually be happening?* I thought.

The witch doctor stood between the two boys, nodding his head up and down, as if to answer my question.

"And you boys have told him how to become a child of God?" I probed.

"Yes, we told him, 'Raise your hands up to Heaven, and surrender to God, and ask Jesus to be your Savior, and He will also be your Brother, and His Father will also be your Father.'" Again, the witch doctor nodded, as I stood in awe, trying to comprehend it all.

"Brother Levi, we need your help," they said. "We noticed that you have scissors in your house. Do you think you could cut this man's hair?"

What a relief! I thought from within. "Yes, in fact, I could cut the fetishes off his neck as well," I offered.

As I began cutting this new believer's hair, many thoughts went through my mind, and I knew that I had to make some serious changes in my thinking. That evening, something happened as I went to my knees, asking God to forgive my unbelief, and for His Holy Spirit to come upon me. Suddenly, a marvelous peace came over me, and His power flowed in to help me believe that "with God all things are possible" (Matt. 19:26b), and that "without faith it is impossible to please Him" (Heb. 11:6a). From that day forward, I knew that things would never be the same, and that I could never again embrace the doctrine of Cessation Theology.

As I began to search the Scriptures again, more strength and faith came to me. I started to read the Scriptures as they were, through the eyes of a new believer; and in doing so, I found no biblical support for believing that the gifts had ceased, or that they were only for the apostles, as I had been previously taught.

And why had I been told that the baptism of the Holy Spirit was not for today? There was nothing to support it. I knew that from that evening onward, I was different inside, and I began to understand many things that I hadn't understood before. Thank God for my humble African teachers.

Beloved reader, this life of following Jesus is a marvelous adventure. He has said,

> *All power is given unto Me in heaven and in earth. Go ye therefore, and teach all nations, baptizing them in the name of the Father, and of the Son, and of the Holy Ghost: teaching them to observe all things whatsoever I have commanded you: and, lo, I am with you always, even unto the end of the world* (Matthew 28:18b-20).

You might be saying, "But I am not called to be a missionary." Oh, yes, you are! You might not be called to go across the ocean, or even across the country, but you are called to go across the street. Yet many Christians today do not even know the names of their neighbors on either side of them, or across the street. Sometimes it is easier to stick with old friends across town. Could it be that the garage door opener has made it easier to drive straight in to our houses to avoid being bothered by potential nosey neighbors? We must not forget those around us who are dying without Christ. Let us remember that indeed, we are our "brother's keeper" (see Gen. 4:9-10).

We pray that as you read on, more than anything else, the love of Jesus will fill your heart, and the desire to serve Him will be born within you.

Chapter Three

THE MAN IN A CAGE

⚓

Many years ago, I was told of a young man named José, who was kept in a cage by his parents on the coast of the southern state of Oaxaca in Mexico. At that time, we were living in Guatemala. José was so wild and bound with demons that his parents had built a special cage of concrete and steel, by order of the local police. There he had spent the previous 15 years, similar to the man of the Gadarenes (see Luke 8:26-39).

When I heard this story, I felt compassion for this boy, and planned to go to see him during my next trip to Mexico. But first, there was fasting and praying. As time passed, the feeling of urgency to go to this young man only increased within me, and I thought, *How must his parents feel? What if he were my son? What a terrible thing to be forced to put your own son in a cage! And 15 years at that!*

The day came, and I arrived at the house of José's parents early in the morning. The cage could be seen from the street, and inside of it, this poor victim of satan was pacing back and forth, totally naked, with long hair and overgrown fingernails and toenails. José would not accept clothing or take a bath. The floor was his toilet. Anything given to him for his comfort was torn up, destroyed, and thrown out of the cage. The odors, which reached the street, were almost unbearable.

Although his mother had already gone to the market, I found the father at home. Upon talking with him, I discovered that he possessed a faith in Christ, and soon I was granted permission to go to José's cage and speak with him. I was glad that I had not eaten breakfast that morning. In my heart, I prayed not only for José, but also for grace to get closer to that strong, foul smell.

"José," I said, "I'm Brother Levi." His face was saying, "Be gone!" but not a word came out of his mouth. As I began to speak of the love of Jesus to him, his countenance grew angrier, until finally, he sat on the dirty concrete floor with his legs crossed, and stuffed his fingers into his ears. My mind went back years prior to the experience of the African boys with the witch doctor. The holy name of Jesus is all-powerful in any age, and as on other occasions since, I knew that satan had to go. I began ordering him to open those ears and hear the command to leave José's body that very moment. Consequently, I began to see changes in José as he started to cough out the spirits that had occupied his body and mind.

Then he arose and came straightway to the door of the cage, asking, "Who are you?" Once again, I stated my name, and began to tell him about the love of Jesus for him, and how He gave His life to save him. The tears began to flow from his eyes, and it was clear that the Holy Spirit was reaching his heart and bringing this dear lost soul to our Savior. The words of Jesus came to me, "All that [those whom] the Father giveth Me shall come to Me; and him that cometh to Me I will in no wise cast out" (John 6:37). What rejoicing there must have been in Heaven, and I could feel it within my heart as well.

The tears ran down José's cheeks and dropped on his bare feet. As the transformation of a new birth was taking place within, José put both of his hands over his heart and said, "I feel so happy!" I will never forget that moment. It was sunrise within! The clouds of darkness and torment were blown away. Jesus was now on the throne in his heart, and satan had been thrown out. All things were new.

"José," I said, "put your hands between the bars. I want to cut your nails," and I took out my nail clippers. "And now, your feet below the door." Then turning to his father, I asked him for the key to let José out.

"The key?" he asked. "We lost the key years ago."

"Then bring me a hammer, if you have one," I said.

He hurried into the house and came back with a hammer. The lock had become rusted, but with several hits, it broke open, and we let José out. He wanted a bath and went into a little room where there was a barrel of water. I handed him a bag of laundry detergent, and went out to my car to look for a pair of pants and a shirt in my suitcase. Soon José emerged bathed, dressed, and in his right mind. I was waiting for him with my barber shears, which I had brought by faith. While sitting in the chair to have his long hair cut off, his face glowed with the joy of his love for Jesus.

It was as we were learning some Christian songs together that José's mother returned from the market. Upon seeing the open cage and having no knowledge of what had happened, she shouted, "Oh no! José has escaped!"

"No," I assured her. "Here he is. Here is your son!"

She stood still in near unbelief, and finally asked with hesitation, "Is it you, José?"

"Yes, Mother. Jesus has freed me and saved me, and He has made me so happy!"

Carmen, his mother, could say no more, but ran to embrace him. These were unforgettable moments, and all of our eyes were filled with tears.

José needed shoes, and because mine didn't fit him, we walked to the open market later that day where there were many styles of sandals to choose from. As he was trying on a pair, the lady who owned the business pulled me aside and said, "This boy seems familiar. Would he be any relation to the boy in the cage across the way?"

"This is José, the one who was in the cage," I answered. "God has saved and transformed him."

She stood there speechless and astonished. And I was given the perfect opportunity to speak to her of God's saving, healing, and delivering power. When we tried to pay her for the sandals, she wouldn't take the money. "Please wear the sandals with blessing," she said to him.

As we walked out of the market, I said to José, "Now, let's walk over to a little evangelical church. I want you to meet Pastor Pablo." Pablo was a new pastor, fresh out of seminary, 27 years old, with a small family. As we approached the church, he was just coming out of his house, which was next door. We greeted each other, and then I asked him if he had heard about the boy in the cage.

"Oh, yes," he exclaimed. "How sad it is. I need to go over and see him!"

With that, I stepped aside, and presented José. "You won't need to. I have brought him to you, and he needs a pastor."

Pablo reached out and embraced José, and soon both were in tears.

Before we turned to leave, Pablo asked, "Brother Levi, when will you be coming this way again?"

"Next month, November, God willing. I am having meetings under a thatched roof in the coast town of Huatulco," I replied. "Would you like to go? It is for three days."

"Could you come by for us?"

"Yes, of course, I will." And so it was arranged.

The next month, Pablo and his wife, Silvia, and small daughter accompanied us to the little thatch church in Huatulco. On the first evening of our meetings, over one hundred people were present, all new believers, many from a life of deep sin. Previously, we had prayed much for God's Spirit to move upon them and lead them into a life of victory. As the evening moved on, I could see on their faces that many were surrendering all to Jesus, and that satan was losing his stronghold in their lives.

As the meeting was coming to a close, suddenly a demon spirit in a woman screeched with an ear piercing scream, as they often do when they are losing the "house" they reside in. Knowing what would happen next, I ran to cushion her fall off the bench. Then a few more came forth screaming. This caused the demonic spirits in two others to become nervous, and they, too, began to scream, with the same result of falling off the bench. We continued to run and cushion them; however, Pastor Pablo became nervous and fled out to the sidewalk. He walked around the block until we were finished with 22 deliverances, at two in the morning. His wife and daughter, however, had remained until all 22 were freed from demonic power. I was especially glad for the help of Eduardo, the pastor of that little church. It was his first experience, and he has since become a strong warrior against satan over the last 20 years.

The next morning, after breakfast, Pablo came to my side and expressed his regret for not having helped with the deliverances.

He then explained his need to also be freed from satan's power. So while we prayed with him in a separate room and he made confessions to the Lord, the powers of darkness began to manifest, even as the demons were uprooted. As he lay on the bed, he experienced great pain throughout his body as they came forth a few at a time, pulling and tearing at his muscles and tendons. Soon, most were gone, except for a few that had moved quickly to hide out in his feet, causing his feet to cramp and curl up tight. They eventually had to depart from there also, in the name of Jesus. It was a strenuous struggle for Pablo, and he was unable to get up for a while. But when he did, the Holy Spirit took control of his life, and everything was different. Since that time, God has enlarged his ministry, and he is free from satan's power.

Chapter Four

A DIVINE DELAY

⚓

In 1994, as we headed back to our home in Guatemala, we were informed of some disappointing news while in a small town on the Mexican side of the border. We would not be able to cross over into Guatemala that day, because it was a holiday. Furthermore, we would have to renew our visas. At first, we felt discouraged, considering that we were being hindered from reaching our destination and would have to spend the weekend in that little town. But as I thought about our circumstances and realized that there was little I could do, a peace entered my heart, and the Lord directed us to seek our brothers and sisters in Christ in that place. After a time of sweet fellowship, we found ourselves ministering in a church on Sunday evening.

During the meeting, the Spirit of the Lord moved in hearts, and we found faith present and the freedom to invite those who needed prayer for healing or deliverance to remain afterwards. There were 11 people who stayed. As Lily and I ministered to them one at a time, we saw many healings and people set free. Finally, we reached the last one, who had been waiting patiently, a lady about 60 years old. Her daughter had been leading her by the hand, and now helped her to be seated on the chair in front of us. As we talked with her, we discovered that she was totally blind and had been so for many years.

We had learned from prior experiences that nothing is too hard for the Lord; consequently, we leave the results to Him. Believe me, there have been times when the devil has tried to intimidate us, saying, "You'll never see this one healed!" And sometimes we haven't seen the healing. Truly, it can affect you, if you let it. However, we have decided to take all cases, head on, and to trust the Lord for the results. If we don't see positive results, we are challenged to search our own hearts first, to determine if the problem is in us.

It is customary for me to ask the same question of anyone who seeks healing: "Do you believe that God is going to heal you right now?" Some of the answers include:

1. "I don't know." These people don't receive healing.

2. "I hope so." These don't receive healing either.

3. "If God wills." Most of these people aren't healed.

4. "Yes." These receive healing, for our Lord said, "Let your yea be yea" (see Matt. 5:37). Therefore, don't let your "yea" be "I hope so."

I asked our blind sister in Christ, "Margarita, do you believe that Jesus will give you your eyesight right now?" When she firmly responded, "Yes," we knew she would be healed. After prayer was made and the spirit of blindness was commanded to leave her, she opened her eyes, leaving the world of darkness behind saying, "I can see everything perfectly!"

A young man from the U.S., who was seated to my right, was quite amazed and asked, "Really?"

"Yes," she replied, "and I can see your blue eyes!"

He was the only one in the church with blue eyes, and she had never seen him before.

We thank our Lord for the delay in travel and our stay in that little town. With God, there are no mistakes. The encounters of this life are for a divine, eternal purpose, and for God's glory. Let us face them patiently and with acceptance, or we may lose eternal opportunities and eternal rewards as well.

I take this moment to say to the young man from the U.S., "The next time you look into the mirror and see those blue eyes that God gave you, remember the miracles that God did for Margarita, and be assured that our Savior also sees into your eyes and wants you to serve Him."

Chapter Five

CHRISTIANS WITH DEMONS

⚓

I know that many of you who read this chapter title are already wondering, *How can this be? A Christian with demon spirits?* "Impossible," you say.

Please listen carefully, as I explain. We have seen the power of God's Spirit at work in Christians by the supreme authority of the name of Jesus hundreds of times over, in many countries. Nevertheless, many well-meaning people will reason that a Christian cannot be possessed by demons, because possession implies ownership. Therefore, it is not *possession*, but rather they define it as *oppression*.

POSSESSION VERSUS OWNERSHIP

Well, first, let's clarify that *possession* does not *imply ownership*. It only implies *possession*. Let's say you own a house, and you rent it out. Then one day, you decide that you yourself want to move into it, but the renter does not want to move out. The house is not his; he

is not the owner, yet he is in possession of it. He stubbornly refuses to move. He knows that he has no legal right to be there,
but he is hoping that you will become tired of asking him to
leave. If you want to pursue your case, you must go to a judge
and get an eviction notice with an official signature by the
judge. If the tenant refuses still, then the sheriff will be sent to
throw him out. Do not be misled by the often heard expression:
"Possession implies ownership." It does not.

When we meet a believer who recognizes that his life is being
controlled by powers, which he has been unable to cope with (also
called compulsive behavior), we realize there are demons involved. We also know that an eviction notice, signed by Jesus, is
what is needed. This is the legal authority that satan's emissaries
must obey. Sometimes, we meet a fortress of demonic spirits in
one person; much prayer and often fasting are needed to remove
them all. But in any case, we are guaranteed the victory.

I will deal with many unanswered questions about deliverance
in a coming book, but meanwhile, it is necessary to clarify this
matter of Christians with demons.

BODY, SOUL, BUT NOT THE SPIRIT

Once during my conversation with a director of a seminary in
another country, he came against me with great anger, arguing,
"You are a heretic! How can the Holy Spirit live with a demon in
the same body?"

I felt the Holy Spirit giving me an answer within: "How can the
Holy Spirit live with you or with me?" This raised his temperature
and the color of his face, and he still would not be convinced.

Many times, people use the text in First John 5:18 as the basis
of their argument: "We know that whosoever is born of God sin-
neth not; but he that is begotten of God keepeth himself, and that
wicked one toucheth him not." Then we are told, "See, there you

have it! A Christian cannot be touched by satan; he cannot be possessed!"

Let's look more carefully at this text. We are made by our Creator in a tripartite way: body, soul, and spirit. The body is our house. It is the first thing we see as we look at one another. But the "real you" is on the inside; that is your spirit. We can use an example of three circles. The outer circle represents the body, the next circle inward is the soul, and the very inner circle is the spirit, where one dwells, and where God's Spirit dwells when a person receives the Lord as Savior.

We are told in the Word that when the Spirit of God comes into us, He seals us unto the day of redemption (see Eph. 1:13-14; 2 Cor. 1:22). The seal means that He who is in there will not break it and come out, nor can he who would like to come in, break in and enter. Satan would like to invade the area of the real you, where the Holy Spirit lives, but he cannot do so. However, he can convince us to live in disobedience to God's Word. Then he has legal ground to move his agents into the body and soul area. With most sins, the body and soul are closely tied together, which brings compulsive behavior into operation.

Deliverance is not possible without conviction of sin, repentance, and confession. Many people want these changes, but they need help from the family of God. However, the family of God, being entertained by more "pleasant" doctrines, continues to relegate these hurting, needy individuals to "professionals and medications," which actually serve to make satan's agents comfortable. Consequently, more room is made for additional spirits to come into the soul area through lust, anxiety, avarice, or any other thing which the enemy uses to war against us. Then they move into the body area to cause further distress—sicknesses and nervous disorders. While the believer is sealed in the spirit area where demons cannot enter, he nevertheless can be enslaved by evil spirits, surrounding him on all sides. Hence, this person needs to be freed, and when he is, he shall be free indeed.

The thought life is usually the first place the enemy hits. If he can gain access to our thoughts, he can surround our spirit, making us unable to function in our spiritual lives for the Lord. The Holy Spirit is within, and He is grieved. He wants to expand His territory to the soul and body area, but if we are enjoying a certain sin in one of those areas, He will not invade you. If you or I, by disobedience, have allowed ourselves to be invaded by satan's agents, because of having succumbed to his temptations, then we must suffer the consequence until we are ready to repent. The Holy Spirit will wait for you. He will not fill us, or act against our will. He respects our right to choose. But He will be right there to help us when we decide to repent and abandon the sin.

SEALED BY THE HOLY SPIRIT

Now, let's return to why the enemy cannot touch the child of God. That child has a seal upon his spirit. If we live in obedience to God's Word, then we are also protected in these other two areas. We, by obedience in turning our bodies over to Him as a living sacrifice, holy and acceptable unto God, which is our reasonable service, can expect to be transformed daily by the renewing of our minds, by the Spirit of God and the Word of God, and can begin to prove what is that good and acceptable, and perfect will of God (see Rom. 12:1-2).

Perhaps you can visualize the plan of the tabernacle, which was given to Moses, for Israel. The tabernacle consisted of three areas: the outer courtyard (representing the body), the Holy Place (representing the soul), and the Holy of Holies (representing the spirit). The Holy of Holies is also the place where God lives (within your spirit, the real you). He made it understood that anyone entering the Holy of Holies of the tabernacle would face the penalty of death, with the exception of the High Priest, once a year, with the blood. Likewise, our spirit is sealed by the Holy Spirit. God's Spirit will not allow satan or his agents to enter into that area. He cannot enter there, where the "real you" lives. However, he can, with our permission, reach into the soul and body areas.

In the Holy Place, that second area (the soul), there were three pieces of furniture: the table of showbread, the golden lampstand, and the alter of incense. These three correspond to the three areas of the soul: the will, the intellect, and the emotions. In our coming book on deliverance, we will explain these more clearly.

Chapter Six

WHAT DID JESUS DO?

⚓

We are to obey the Great Commission, which means to invade satan's territory and seek the lost sheep who belong to the Lord. Jesus said, "No man can come to Me, except the Father which hath sent Me draw him" (John 6:44a). He also said, "All that the Father giveth Me shall come to Me" (John 6:37a).

In the prayer of our Lord to His Father, recorded in John chapter 17, we hear our Lord saying seven (7) times, the phrase, "those whom Thou hast given Me," declaring that we, yes, we ourselves, are the Father's gift to the Son. And He needs us to bring in the remaining gifts, who are scattered around the globe—some in Africa, others in Asia or Indonesia, and some in your own neighborhood.

JESUS DID THREE THINGS

So often we hear the expression, "What would Jesus do?" However, it is more appropriate to ask, "What *did* Jesus do?" As you carefully read the four Gospels—Matthew, Mark, Luke, and John—you will find Him doing essentially three things: preaching, healing, and casting out demons. He did these same three things over and over again. Can you imagine how many people would have believed on Him, if He had only preached? Probably very few, if any.

He said to the disciples, and says to us: "As My Father hath sent Me, even so send I you" (John 20:21b). That is, as the Father sent Jesus the Son, preaching His Word, healing the sick, and casting out demons, even so, He sends us to do the same.

Then we find in the Book of Acts, the disciples doing the same three things. Today it is not so important to think about what would Jesus do; but rather, what *did* He do? And why are we not doing these things today? The most frequent answer to this question is because that dispensation is over; the days of miracles ceased with the apostles. This answer is the essence of the Cessation Theology. The problem is, there is not a speck of support for it in the Scriptures. We must not build our theology upon our ideas or reasoning. The Lord has said to us, "My thoughts are not your thoughts" (Isa. 55:8a); and "lean not unto thine own understanding" (Prov. 3:5b).

DYING TO SELF TO DO GREATER THINGS

Indeed, there have been many wonderful moves of God's Spirit, including miracles in the Book of Acts. However, there was a time of revival much greater still in Wales, starting in 1904. And whom did God use so mightily? Evan Roberts, a young man, just 20 years old. People arrived from all over the world to come under the power of God. It was called the "Children's Revival," and no doubt, became the greatest revival in history. So many healings took place that even many officials of Parliament in England took leave to attend the meetings in Wales so that they too could be healed.

The power of God flowing in Wales was so great that a spark from it ignited in the heart of a black man in Texas, named William Seymour. God knew whom to touch, and Seymour went to Los Angeles where the Spirit of God began to move in an old building on Azusa Street, which ignited the flame of the worldwide missionary movement, still continuing today.

However, the flame in most places has gone down, and the embers need to be fanned anew. Moreover, we cannot work ourselves up to it. Rather, there must first be a complete death to self. The Spirit of God and His work cannot be brought about by our efforts toward excellence. For example, in many churches today, water baptism is being used for testimony of faith and for church membership. It is not intended for either one. Water baptism is a vow, a pact with God of death to self. This is where we start. Many have gotten simply wet, but have made no vow to our Lord, who died for us. In true water baptism, we vow to Him to die to ourselves once and for all. Paul gave us the words of that vow in Galatians 2:20, "I am crucified with Christ: nevertheless I live; yet not I, but Christ liveth in me: and the life which I now live in the flesh I live by the faith of the Son of God, who loved me, and gave Himself for me." These are strong words of promise, an oath to God. Yet we find churches requiring people to be re-baptized in order to become members of that particular church, defining baptism as something other than was intended by the Holy Spirit.

Though the days of commercial faith are here, we still have the truth of God's Word and the Holy Spirit as our teacher. We still have the precious promises of our Lord to give us the power of the river of His Spirit flowing from our innermost being, to do the things that He did, to speak with authority and power, and to heal the souls of people everywhere. And we are to do even greater things, as He said, because He would go to the Father, and send us His Holy Spirit. It would not be of us; it must not be of us. It must be Jesus, glorified by the Holy Spirit, because we have died to self, and our lives are now hidden with Christ in God.

A PERSONAL SHIFT IN FAITH

Over 40 years ago I went to Africa. Although I struggled with the language, I eventually managed to bring several souls to our Savior. They were in earnest about serving Jesus, and even began performing the miracles that I couldn't do—a perplexing and embarrassing situation. It suddenly occurred to me the reason why this was happening. In their simple faith, they were reading the Scriptures just like they are written, without any interpretation. I had enough of the language at that point to explain salvation, but not enough to explain the Cessation Theology. Praise God! He kept me from ruining their beautiful, childlike faith! He truly had enrolled me in a far more important school than I had ever been before, and I am eternally grateful. For I saw what He would do if we would only believe. Let's listen to what Jesus said to Martha: "Said I not unto thee, that, if thou wouldest believe, thou shouldest see the glory of God?" (John 11:40b).

> *Oftentimes, we are accused by fellow believers, of following after signs. Truly, we do not follow the signs. Rather, the signs follow us. Jesus said, "And these signs shall follow them that believe; In My name shall they cast out devils; they shall speak with new tongues; they shall take up serpents; and if they drink any deadly thing, it shall not hurt them; they shall lay hands on the sick, and they shall recover"* (Mark 16:17-18).

Little by little, the Lord reshaped my thinking. As I look back and see the damage that the Cessation Theology did to my faith, I am very grateful to our Lord for showing me these truths, in spite of my ignorance. But there is one thing that I must confess. I did not believe in the gift of tongues for today, and it wasn't until being in the Lord's work for about 18 years that I changed my mind. It happened at a crisis time in my life.

During a long period of prayer, the Lord was very near, and I wanted Him nearer still. I had no idea what was about to happen, but suddenly I began to pray in another tongue, something I had never sought. I felt a barrier removed as if I had suddenly been aligned with the Holy Spirit. My heart was warmed, and my spirit edified and filled with the joy of His presence. Then He made known to me the meaning of what the Spirit was speaking. It was a real milestone in my life. Truthfully, I had never wanted to speak in tongues, because I had seen so many distasteful demonstrations in churches. But the Lord overruled all that, and has since shown me that it is important not to allow anyone else's negative experiences or the enemy to discourage what the Spirit of God wants to do for us. Since that day, my life has been different in so many ways, and it is easier to come boldly before the throne of grace. Thank You, Lord Jesus.

Rivers of Living Water

The Father continues to speak of the "river" that should flow in you and me. Will you listen to His words as He delivers them to His servant:

My Child, did you know
    That Living Waters from My Throne do flow?
Beloved Child, these Rivers need a place to go,
    A tender broken heart below,
Someone whose "yea is yea," and "no is no."
    Someone who is ready to know
His sins are washed as white as snow
    By the blood of My Son,

Jesus, the most loving One.
    It matters not what you have done.

So let me hear you say below,
    "Lord, in me, let Your Rivers flow;
For I will Your channel be,
    Then, they Your loving Son can see."
And you will begin to know
    How grace and love can grow
And in the darkest places glow.
    These Rivers that from My throne do flow
Are looking for a heart below.

Many have heard it, and they do know;
    But still they have not come to think
How much I long for them to drink.
    To drink of Me, the River above,
For I am God, and I am Love.
    A drink that starts the River to flow,
And no one knows where it will go,
    Or how My glory I will show,
Or how many saints I'll cause to grow.
    I speak to you, My Child below,
In you My love I want to show.

Rivers? Yes, Rivers from here above,
    Where I am God, and I am Love.
Doubt Me not, or you'll never know
    What I can do through you below.
A River through your tongue can go,
    And also through your hands may flow.
And don't forget about your feet
    As they walk upon the street.

They are Rivers, showing you where to go.
    Will you let My Rivers flow
Through an open heart below?

My Rivers, you cannot make them flow,
   Nor can you tell them where to go.
In them I have put My power
   And there will never be an hour
When Living Waters will not flow
   Through human hearts on earth below.

Yes, He has "rivers," for He has already told us, "He that believeth on Me…out of His belly shall flow rivers of living water" (John 7:38).

There is an urgency today for rivers of living water to flow to needy hearts all over this earth. The daytime is far advanced, and the night is coming upon us.

TAKE UP YOUR CROSS

The prophet, Elisha, was careful, steadfast, and obedient in all things, in order to receive the double portion of Elijah's spirit. When he saw that his servant, Gehazi, had fallen into the trap of covetousness, he reproved him, saying, "Is it a time to receive money, and to receive garments, and oliveyards, and vineyards, and sheep, and oxen, and menservants, and maidservants?" (2 Kings 5:26).

If we want to be a clean channel for the river of God's Spirit to flow through us, then we must take heed to these words. The Lord wants clean channels, and some of them will be financial channels, blessing God's work around the world. However, let us beware of the leprous sin of avarice, where the love of money and other material things creeps into the heart. The material blessings that God bestows must continue to flow through our hands to where God intends them to go. If we allow covetousness to penetrate our hearts, together with the love of comfort, it will turn into spiritual leprosy, just as it did with Gehazi.

The God of all comfort, for the joy that was set before Him, endured the cross. He asks us also to deny ourselves (lay aside comfort whenever necessary) and take up our cross daily, and follow Him (see Heb. 12:2; Luke 9:23). We should daily deny ourselves and daily bear our cross. Our cross, not His cross.

If you have been baptized by water, did you understand the vow of death to self, and are you daily bearing your cross? Or was it simply a testimony of joining a church? Indeed, to be a member of a local church that preaches all the truth of the Word of God can be a source of many blessings. However, the real purpose of baptism is lost if it is used for acquiring members.

HE IS WITH US NOW

The Spirit of God is ready to move mightily in fast flowing rivers through us, in a manner never seen before, as at Pentecost, in Wales, and Azusa Street, and even much more. And there are places around the globe that are experiencing revival and great masses of souls are coming to Jesus; however, it is still a small percentage. Still, something is missing, and much pride remains in our hearts, while churches have held on to denominational differences.

A partial fulfillment of the prophecy of Joel, as quoted by Peter in Acts 2:14-21 was seen in the early Church days. Now, the greater part of that prophecy, not yet seen, is about to come to pass. This is the reason that the Holy Spirit has guided this book into your hands. Through you, and others like you, He will pour out His Spirit on people everywhere (see Acts 2:17). Will you deny yourself, putting love of comfort and of things aside? You might not even have to get rid of them. Just keep them out of your heart.

This short life He has given us here on earth is our opportunity to prove our love to Him. It will soon be past. Consider 70 years, approximately 25,000 days—how will you use them? They are flying past us, and soon, we will "fly away," as the psalmist David says. This is the moment to remake your vow with the Lord, who made us and died for us. The Holy Spirit is waiting to bless you, and fill you. It is a life of continuous blessing, when we are obedient, a life of daily communion with the Father, and with the Son, through the Holy Spirit. It is a life of experiencing His love, His joy, and His peace every day.

Listen to these precious words of our Lord: "If a man love Me, he will keep My words: and My Father will love him, and We will come unto him, and make Our abode with him" (John 14:23). The proof of our love for Him is obedience. The outcome of our love for Him is the reality of the love of the Father and the Son for us, and the beauty of Their presence with us, right now, not just in Heaven. Right now, Their dwelling place can be with you! Heaven on earth, wherever you are!

He said, "Go ye into all the world" (Mark 16:15). That means, go across the street, and go across town, or go across the ocean. Jesus is real; He is present; and He has said, "Lo, I am with you always" (Matt. 28:20).

We read in John 1:32 that Jesus received the Holy Spirit upon Him in the form of a dove. But He did not come upon the disciples in that form, but rather in the form of tongues of fire (see Acts 2:1-4), as prophesied in Luke 3:16, "...He shall baptize you with the Holy Ghost and with fire."

> *The rivers bring cleansing and life. The fire brings the power and total removal of all that is not eternal. We have all that we need, and what's more, this wonderful promise: "Behold, I give unto you power to tread on serpents and scorpions, and over all the power of the enemy: and nothing shall by any means hurt you. Notwithstanding in this rejoice not, that the spirits are subject unto you; but rather rejoice, because your names are written in heaven" (Luke 10:19-20).*

Chapter Seven

A VISIT TO EUROPE

⚓

Our names…written in Heaven! Glory! This floods our hearts with joy. My wife and I have been blessed to serve the Lord with abundant joy for many years, and even though trials have often come that could have been overwhelming, He has made us more than conquerors, and we can only praise Him. We trust that He will continue to give us health and sufficient strength to go to many more nations.

In the year 2003, the Lord revealed that we should travel to four countries in Europe, namely, France, England, Spain, and Holland…and in that order.

Part of our plan in France was to meet with a special brother in Paris, whom God had saved and healed of several infirmities, which he had suffered in the communist country where I had originally met him. We were rejoicing with him that he had found freedom in Christ, freedom from several diseases, and now, freedom from the slavery of communism. It was a thrill to our hearts to pray with Ramon, and to see him filled to overflowing with the joy of the Holy Spirit.

After spending six days in a hotel in Paris, we discovered that funds were not coming in as we had expected, and our faith was being tried. We could not afford to stay another day in the hotel; neither did we have enough money to go anywhere else. Furthermore, it was raining outside. As we sat at a little round table, eating a light breakfast that the hotel offered, my wife and I just looked at each other. We had to turn in the key to our room by 11:00 A.M. and remove our bags. But where would we go? There was only one place to go, and that was to our heavenly Father.

Of course, these are truths we know, but we would rather not have to endure such trials to prove them. As we finished our prayers together, our minds went to the phone card that we had bought in Europe. There were still a few minutes of use left on it, so we dialed our dear friend and sister in Christ, Hanna, in the U.S., who serves so faithfully as bookkeeper for our mission, Berean Bible Fellowship.

"Hanna, we are in Paris. Have we received any gifts of money recently?" we asked.

"Yes, an unusual blessing of the Lord—one thousand dollars came in just yesterday, and it is already in your account. Try the ATM," she replied.

We hurried down three blocks to the ATM, and there it was! The Lord came through again. Back at the hotel, we were able to squeeze three more minutes out of the phone card, and called our friends, Ron and Julie, in England.

"We are coming to England, Ron. Would it be possible to see you?"

Without hesitation, Ron replied, "It is urgent that you do so."

With that, I answered, "God willing, we'll be there tomorrow morning," wondering what Ron meant by "urgent."

Ron and Julie, now advanced in years, had stayed with us for six months in our home in Guatemala. We had learned to love them and had prayed often for them through the years. They both had received the Lord's touch, and were witnessing the sick recovering under their hands and evil spirits departing, as they used the authority of Jesus' name.

I continued to wonder about the urgency that Ron had mentioned, and in the meantime, Lily and I bought two bus tickets to travel to England that night. I soon discovered how much more French we should have learned as we tried to direct the taxi driver to the proper bus terminal. But God is merciful! We did arrive on time.

The bus then took us directly to the tunnel under the sea. In those days, many people were afraid of a terrorist attack on the tunnel; hence, extra precautions were taken. The wide door on the end of the train opened, and the bus drove inside of it. We never got off until we were on the shores of England, a very fast ride, taking only 25 minutes. From there, we soon found ourselves in London, and then on to our friends' location by another bus, where we were picked up by a man named Peter, Ron and Julie's neighbor. Thank the Lord for good neighbors.

Upon arrival at their home, we were very glad to see them again. But as we spoke, just barely inside the door, I noticed a lump on the right side of Ron's neck.

"This is the urgency I spoke about," Ron mentioned with sadness. "It is cancer. You know that we want to go back to India to teach in a Bible school, as we do each year, but the doctor told me that if I do so this time, I won't ever return to England."

Ron and Julie had dedicated their lives to serving their Lord, showing people that they, too, can do the three things that Jesus did—preach, heal, and cast out demons. Days were truly full for them in India, but now it looked as though they would not be going back.

I felt in my spirit that this was an attack from the enemy to prevent them from returning to India where there would be a mighty outpouring of God's Spirit.

So, Lily and I laid hands on Ron as he sat on a chair in the parlor and Peter sat on the sofa. Julie stood to one side. Asking our Father for wisdom, we followed the leading of the Spirit, who directed me to put my index finger directly on the lump, and say, "Your name is cancer, and you're coming out!"

Immediately a voice spoke up, one that was not Ron's, yet coming out of his mouth, saying, "Don't say that name!"

"What! You don't like to hear your name—cancer?" I repeated again, "Your name is cancer, and you're coming out, in the name of Jesus!"

This time, the response was in the plural: "We are not coming out. We cannot because we have been assigned to keep him from going to India!" they insisted.

"Well, you just lost your assignment. Here is an eviction notice on you, signed by Jesus, so get moving! Out with you!"

Suddenly there were signs of turmoil and groaning, and Ron began to cough heavily for about 12 minutes. During this entire time, I held my finger on the lump, and with each cough, the lump shrunk a little more. Finally, it was completely gone, and has never returned. The next day at the doctor's office, Ron received confirmation that the cancer was gone. So, they immediately bought their tickets for India, and went on to experience the best and most fruitful year of their lives. Once again, together with Ron and Julie, we praise the King of glory! And we know that you, too, Peter, will not forget what you saw and heard that day in September

2003, in the parlor of Ron and Julie's house. The Lord wants to be glorified in what He does. Let us give Him the glory.

Preach, Heal, Cast Out Demons

When our Lord returned from the desert where He was tempted by the devil and before He performed His first miracle, He went into the synagogue in Nazareth where He was raised, and stood up to read from the scroll of the Book of Isaiah:

> *The Spirit of the Lord is upon Me, because He hath anointed Me to preach the gospel to the poor; He hath sent Me to heal the brokenhearted, to preach deliverance to the captives, and recovering of sight to the blind, to set at liberty them that are bruised, to preach the acceptable year of the Lord* (Luke 4:18-19).

Here we see our Lord's agenda. Once again, it is divided into three categories: preaching, healing, and casting out evil spirits—the same three activities we find in all four Gospels, and the same three that the disciples are found doing in the Book of Acts. So what are we to do? Preach. Heal. Cast out evil spirits. These actions are not just the responsibility of ministers and missionaries, but of every believer in Christ.

Let's look again at the words of our Lord: "These *signs* shall follow them that *believe...*" (Mark 16:17-18, emphasis added). Notice that this outcome is to be the norm for believers—all believers. Yet there are those who do not believe in such miracles. They believe in Christ as Savior, but that is as far as they go. Their motto is: "I don't bother satan, and he doesn't bother me." I suspect that with that philosophy, he shouldn't need to. For it is when you begin to snatch souls from the devil's strongholds that he comes against you. Some of the battles we have had against the enemy have been fierce. But we know, as the apostle Paul proclaimed, we are already "more than conquerors through Him that loved us" (Rom. 8:37; see also verses 38-39).

Chapter Eight

ANGELIC HELP

⚓

In the year 1986, in the state of Chiapas, Mexico, a brother in Christ came to me very worried, asking, "Have you heard what the devil has said through the mouth of Señor Gomez?"

"No," I said. "Tell me."

"Well, the demons spoke very angrily, saying, 'We are going to kill that Levi. He is stealing all the souls that belong to us!'"

I simply responded, "God will watch over us as He has promised."

Two nights later, I was returning home on foot. We lived in the country, outside of town, and as I entered the property, it was difficult to see, especially because there was very little moonlight. At first, I thought I saw movement in the bushes. Then suddenly, there was Señor Gomez coming at me with his machete raised over his head.

"This is the end of you!" he shouted, as he ran toward me. There was almost no time to think, and only the words, "Lord Jesus!" came out of my mouth.

Immediately, I saw an amazing thing happen. My attacker crashed into an invisible barrier and fell over backward! Stunned, he got up, wielding his machete, and once again dashed toward me. And again, he crashed into an invisible barrier. Even more startled, he stood again, took time to regain his balance, and then took off running down the road.

Later, he moved out of town and was never seen again. We continue to pray that our Lord will be merciful to him, and bring him to Himself. We trust that Señor Gomez will be another soul that satan will lose.

Be always reminded that "greater is He that is in you, than he that is in the world" (1 John 4:4b). He is a defeated enemy.

He shall give His angels charge over thee…(Psalm 91:11).

Chapter Nine

AN AFRICAN GEM
DISCOVERED IN CUBA

⚓

Since late 1958, I had wanted to go to Cuba with the Gospel. Then, in January 1959, the country fell to communism under Fidel Castro. Consequently, my plans for Cuba were laid aside, until September 1993, when I was able to make the first of 16 trips into that country. Up until that time, we had often prayed that God would put all the necessary contacts in order, and that His purposes would be worked out.

On our first trip, which lasted three weeks, the Spirit of God led me to Antonio, a pastor who invited me to his home, where he, his wife, and I enjoyed the Lord's presence together. One day, while we sat at a little table in their kitchen, I noticed a tall figure standing outside the screen door, and mentioned this to Antonio.

"Oh, that must be Galan," he said. "Would you please let him in?"

As Galan entered the kitchen, I had to look upwards to see his face, which was radiant with a Christ-like smile. Galan introduced himself, a 19-year-old Sudanese, orphaned in the southern Sudan at nine years of age, just ten years prior. He and a group of other orphans his age had fled from the Sudan into Ethiopia, where they were met by Cuban troops who were occupying that country. Many orphans from the Sudan had run away to Ethiopia, as the Muslims entered their villages, killing entire families in the Christian south. Hundreds of them were brought into Cuba.

As we talked, I thought of all the suffering that this young lad had already experienced, and on top of that, he then had to adapt to a communist system, learn the Spanish language, and try to forget the past. As we ate together, I could see that in spite of all he had endured, Galan had learned to trust the Lord for everything. His clothing was neat and clean, although quite worn. The meal was very simple, mainly rice and a few beans, but it was given cheerfully and gratefully received.

As we talked together, Antonio began to unfold more of the story of this unusual, noble African lad, and finally his voice took on a serious tone.

"Brother Levi," he said, "there is something important and urgent that I must tell you. Other Sudanese boys have been sent back to the Sudan where they were shot upon arrival by the Muslim government because they are Christians. Soon Galan will also have to go. This will mean his death, because he will not deny Jesus."

It was a dark moment to hear this news, but Galan didn't waste a minute in saying, "It is all right. I will soon go to Heaven to be with Jesus."

This statement drew me right up off my seat, and I stood to embrace him, quickly protesting, "No! You're not going to Heaven. You're going to Guatemala with me!"

And with that, he said, "Oh, thank you!"

However, Antonio began to regrettably inform me that Galan had no documents whatsoever. Immediately, I realized that I had spoken too soon. But God did not want me to know all the facts, and fortunately, because of my ignorance, a prophecy was given that God would fulfill.

I wish that I could tell you all the details of how God worked a wonderful series of miracles, resulting in Galan's departure from Cuba and a subsequent trip to Guatemala. However, although marvelous, the facts are too risky to publish.

I think the Lord knew that with so many of our children grown up and gone from home, we would need another son to take their place. Since that time, Galan has become a part of our family, attended Bible school in Guatemala, learned to speak English, and married a black Christian from Cuba. They now have two small sons, and in 2006, together they moved to Kenya to serve the Lord.

Galan makes frequent trips into his tribe in the southern Sudan, where he has won many of his people to Jesus. God has also helped him to recall his tribal language, and there is another even more wonderful surprise yet to share—Galan found his mother! She was thought to be dead, but God had kept her alive. For years she had prayed that God would protect her son and bring him back home alive. It was a miracle day, during which over 300 of the tribe came together to celebrate this occasion. All day and even all week, tears of joy were shed. People from everywhere came to see for themselves, and to feel him, and re-move any doubts they had about whether he was truly alive or not. Once again, we recall our Lord's words to Martha, "Did I not say unto you, if you *truly believe*, you will see the glory of God?" (see John 11:25-26).

Galan is willing to die in order to bring his people to Jesus, and they are coming…by the hundreds. What is Galan doing? He is doing what Jesus did—preaching the Gospel, healing the sick, and casting out demons. These three things! Many are sick, and many are oppressed by satan; but people respond everywhere he goes. They are hungry for Jesus. One who sees miracles every day has no use for the Cessation Theology. To Galan, such a system of unbelief is unthinkable.

Now, he wants us to accompany him into the Sudan. This is presently a matter of prayer. Although there has been a peace agreement made in the southern Sudan, it is superficial and very fragile. In any case, God will provide the answer; and in the meantime, we are also praying about going to several other countries in Africa. When a few dedicated believers finally understand that Jesus did three things—not just one—then they begin to do them also, and thus, the harvest multiplies much faster.

DRAW NEAR TO HIS POWER

What would Jesus do today? He would do the same three things He did when He walked the earth. What do *we* need to do? Our Lord has already said that these signs would follow those who believe. Believing starts with recognizing our sinful condition, and asking Jesus to be our Savior. However, believing must not stop there. We must also believe in the very words He spoke, in connection with the signs that He wants to do that will create faith in others.

However, if you believe these things have ceased, obviously there will be no way that they will be accomplished through your life. Even though you are a child of God, saved by grace, you will live in frustration because you are not experiencing what God has promised. This was my situation for many years, until I realized that what I thought was sound doctrine was actually unbelief. Since then, the Holy Spirit has been shedding light upon more and more areas of my life where I have lacked faith. I had continued to think in the natural realm without understanding the change that the Holy Spirit was trying to make.

Often we assume that the Holy Spirit has total control of our lives, that we are totally sold out to Him, and that one day, things will get better for us. However, this does not happen automatically. The Word says, "Draw nigh to God, and He will draw nigh to you" (James 4:8a). We must take the first step toward Him, whether we feel like it or not. Then He takes a step toward us. Another step toward Him, and He takes another toward us. James 4:10 expresses it another way: "Humble yourselves in the sight of the Lord, and He shall lift you up." Notice, we take the step of humbling ourselves, and He takes the step of lifting us up toward Him.

But what does humbling ourselves involve?

1. "Cleanse your hands, ye sinners" (James 4:8b). What have you been doing with your hands?

2. "Purify your hearts, ye double minded" (James 4:8b). Are you something else on the inside than what you represent on the outside? Has money, with which God intends to bless you and others, turned into filthy lucre?

3. "Be afflicted, and mourn, and weep: let your laughter be turned to mourning, and your joy to heaviness" (James 4:9). Are we always looking to natural things as our source of joy?

Our Lord has said, "The truth shall make you free" (John 8:32b). Not just the truth that comes from His mouth, but the truth that needs to come from our mouths—the truth about us. David, in Psalm 139:23-24, understood his need to search for the truth inwardly, when he said, "Search me, O God, and know my heart: try me, and know my thoughts: and see if there be any wicked way in me, and lead me in the way everlasting." Every area of ourselves must die. To accomplish Christ's work, both in word and deed, we need only the Christ-life within. This old flesh nature must be crucified daily, or it will start to rise up again. If we die to self today, Jesus can be raised in us today, with resurrection power.

> *That I may know Him, and the power of His resurrection, and the fellowship of His sufferings, being made conformable unto His death* (Philippians 3:10).

The power of His resurrection is what we *desire*, and what we *need*; however, we cannot start with resurrection power. We must first be made conformable to His death, with a willingness to continue through the fellowship of His sufferings; and in the process, the power of His resurrection will begin to work within us.

Let us invite the Holy Spirit to search us on a daily basis, as it is necessary to know the condition of our hearts. Paul further assures,

> *But if the Spirit of Him that raised up Jesus from the dead dwell in you, He that raised up Christ from the dead shall also quicken your mortal bodies by His Spirit that dwelleth in you* (Romans 8:11).

Chapter Ten

MORE MIRACLES IN CUBA

⚓

MORE POWERFUL THAN THE
MEDICAL PROFESSION

The Spirit of God was again leading me. This time it was to visit one of the largest hospitals in Havana, Cuba, to pray for the sick. A Cuban brother, Enrique, accompanied me, and we spent the entire day going from bed to bed.

And the Lord was doing wonderful things. Most of those who received healing also gave their hearts to Jesus. Finally, toward evening, as we were leaving, we saw a lady on a bed set off to one side, for whom we had not prayed. We were tired and hungry, and our feet sore. Worse still, we had yet to walk home in the dark at the risk of being robbed or mugged. But we couldn't resist the Holy Spirit's pull.

As we spoke with her, we discovered that she was a believer, but was totally paralyzed and had been in bed for 11 years! We began anointing her limbs with oil, starting with her feet and legs, and speaking to the paralysis, in the name of Jesus, to leave immediately. First her feet and toes began to move. Then she was able to lift one leg, then the other. I looked around. A few nurses had gathered to watch, as they had never seen her do this before.

Then we went to her arms, anointing them, thanking the Lord for the healing He was about to give, and commanding the paralysis out, in Jesus' name. They responded in the same way, and soon she asked us to pull her up. As she sat on the edge of the bed and continued to pray, once again we noticed there were more nurses still, who formed a circle to watch.

A short while later, she asked for her clothes because she wanted to go home. As they helped her get dressed, we wanted to preach a lengthy message to the nurses, but had to limit it to a few chosen words: "You have seen what Jesus can do, and He also says to you today, that He loves you so much that whoever of you believes on Him, you shall not perish, but shall have everlasting life." We had to leave quickly, but noticed the tears in several eyes. As we made our exit, two nurses also left, walking home with the former patient. She has been in fine health ever since.

Upon exiting the hospital, we found that it was now dark outside, but we felt the presence of the Lord as we hurried home to Enrique's house. Shortly after our arrival, two doctors appeared at the door, and Enrique invited them in. One of them, Ramon, had apparently seen what had taken place at the hospital and also wanted to be healed. He and I went into another room together, where he told me his life story and how he was suffering from epilepsy and diabetes. Both diseases had reached the point of causing a major crisis in his life, preventing him from functioning in a normal manner.

The Lord gave these words of prophecy, "Today you will be rid of all sickness. God loves you, and wants to heal you and save you." We have learned that when the Holy Spirit is urging certain words, they need to be said, for these words produce faith which brings it about. Upon hearing these words, the doctor dropped to his knees, cried out to God, and gave his heart to Jesus. It was one of the most touching scenes I have ever witnessed!

That night, Ramon received total healing from epilepsy and diabetes, and to this day, enjoys good health, another cause for rejoicing by many people. Today he is serving our Lord in other places on the earth. Many wonderful things for God's glory are taking place in Cuba; unfortunately, very little news of these miracles reaches the outside world.

HEALING THROUGH A HAIRCUT

At another time in Cuba, several years ago, I found myself needing a haircut, and knowing of a young barber who cut hair in his home, I went to see him. It was the first time I had been in Rolando's home. He was the only believer in Christ in his family, and that day I had the opportunity to meet his other family members.

When his father came into the room, I instantly felt compassion for him. He was badly bent over and could not straighten up, a condition he had suffered for many years. (I have seen this malady many times in Cuba, especially in Havana.) I asked him if he would allow God to heal him in that moment, and he agreed. Laying one hand on his shoulder, I thanked the Lord for the healing that was about to take place, declared the spirit of infirmity defeated in Jesus' name, and commanded it to come out. He felt something leave his body, and immediately straightened up, to the glory of God!

Even greater than this, that very day salvation came to the entire household—every member gave his or her heart to Jesus. How can I describe the joy that I experience when I see people coming to our

Savior? Truly, we must remember that there is great rejoicing in Heaven amongst the angels over one sinner who repents.

Recently, in certain rural areas of Cuba, there have been many people coming to our Savior, specifically because of the miracles that have been taking place. One entire village has put their faith in Jesus. Why? Because one little obscure congregation took to heart the command of Jesus to go everywhere with the Good News, followed by signs and wonders. Moreover, several churches have been formed because of this obedience.

We wish it were possible to share detailed facts about Cuba, but we cannot mention the real names or places. But, dear reader, please intercede for Cuba and other countries enslaved by communism. You may or may not see the results now, but in Heaven, you will realize the full results of your prayers. You and I have access to the throne of God at all times, and there are no barriers that can remain standing as we take hold of the power and authority that is given to us through the precious blood of Jesus.

Indeed, there have been so many wonderful works of the Lord in Cuba that it would take several pages to write of them.

A Ride on a Bike and a Walk to Heaven

Early one morning while in Havana, a knock came at the door of the house of friends with whom I was staying. It was a lady whom the Lord had healed of cancer the year before.

"Brother Levi," she said, "there is a man at my work who has a four-year-old son. During this last year, his legs became lame. He asked if you could come to my house at nine this morning to pray for him."

My spirit said, "Yes," but my body was craving rest from the activity of the night before. I almost said, "Please tell him that it is better for me in the afternoon," but the Lord said, "You need to go now." So I agreed. As she was leaving, she said, "I will have someone come by for you at 8:30 A.M."

I was ready, and at the right time my driver showed up...on his bicycle! And a homemade bicycle at that—fully equipped with a rack on the back, which I called "the rumble seat." During the 20-minute ride to our destination, my driver swerved between honking cars and zigzagged *most* of the potholes. I found myself praying the whole way for our safety, and that we wouldn't zig when we should zag. To say the least, it was a relief when we arrived. I found not just one man and his son, but instead, a house packed full with people. Two of them hurried out the door to help me off the rack. So kind, they were! They must have been aware of the experience of trying to walk after such a ride. I rubbed my backside and said, "Please, Lord, heal me first."

There was scarcely room to enter the house. Although it was still early in the morning, it was already hot, and there was no extravagance, such as a fan. The Lord led me to speak to them first from His Word. Their eyes showed full attention and spiritual hunger. Then I noticed the father with his little son, and asked him to put the boy in my arms. It had been a year since the child had walked, and the cause of his lameness was still unknown.

Receiving the little one, and knowing that none of those present were yet believers in Christ, I felt it was best to openly thank our heavenly Father for His healing and that they also might know of His love for each of them.

"Father in Heaven, thank You for sending Jesus, Your Son, to this earth to die for us. Thank You for Your great love for us. We now bring this precious little one for Your healing touch. Thank You for the authority You have given us in the name of Jesus, Your Son, and it is in the name of Jesus that we now command all infirmity to leave this child. His legs are now free! He is healed in the name of Jesus!"

The lad began to squirm, and I felt confidence in lowering him to the floor. Immediately, he took off running into the arms of his father, and every eye in that room filled with tears. This rejoicing went on for a while, and then the Holy Spirit impressed me to give an invitation for the people to receive our Savior into their hearts. Everyone in the house, nearly 30 people, did so. We all rejoiced greatly, but I'm sure that there was more rejoicing in Heaven amongst the angels. And it occurred to me, *No wonder they protected me during that bicycle ride!* The rest of the day we witnessed the Lord healing one after another of different infirmities—diabetes, arthritis, asthma, epilepsy, heart congestion, and others. I thank the Lord for giving strength when we have none, for increasing our faith when it is low, for giving His presence as He promised, and for enough grace to make the return trip on that "luxury" bicycle. It was worth it all, and much more.

A TRANSFORMED TRANSMISSION

I want to share one more testimony, though there are dozens equally important.

The following story took place several years ago, on my tenth trip into Cuba, but without the presence of our Lord so real every moment, such an experience would have caused panic.

Along with two Cuban brothers in Christ, we had planned a seven-hour trip to preach the Gospel in the eastern half of Cuba.

When I arrived at the airport in Havana, the two men, Marcos and Roberto, were waiting for me as I came out of the airport at 9:00 P.M. We greeted each other in the love of Christ, and then they helped me carry my bags to the vehicle which would take us eastward to the places we had planned. I had no idea what awaited me and had just assumed that we would travel in a car. But there it was—a huge truck of about a 1950 vintage in a variety of paint colors and rust that had been patched with many scrap pieces of metal.

We were to leave at midnight so that, as much as possible, we could travel undetected. But first, we had to push the truck to get it started. Then we went from place to place within the "black market," purchasing diesel wherever we could find it. People kept it hidden away in barrels and sold it by the liter. Finally, in two hours, we had been able to buy 80 liters of diesel, and were ready by midnight to get on the road, going east.

Roberto had previously worked on the truck for three days in order to get it to run, which left him almost no time to sleep. Yet he drove, and Marcos and I sat with him in the front to keep him awake. However, in less than two hours, Roberto said he could no longer stay awake. The only thing Marcos knew how to drive was a bicycle. So that left me. And I knew it was important to get to our destination before dawn.

The truck had a stick shift with five speeds. I should say, it was five shifts with one speed. But the most difficult part was the steering wheel, which was so loose that it was hard to keep the truck on the road. For about an hour, I managed to battle with the steering wheel, while Roberto was able to get a nap. He then woke up and said that he could do the driving once again.

But soon after Roberto took the wheel, I began to smell smoke, and noticed sparks that could be seen through the holes in the floorboard. Within minutes there were loud, grinding noises, a clash of metal, and the truck began to lose momentum. Suddenly, we heard the sound of something heavy drop to the ground, and we were forced to stop.

We all got out to find that our suspicions were confirmed. The transmission was lying on the ground in a pool of oil. The two Cuban brothers were especially worried about me—an outsider, in the middle of nowhere, without a tourist guide. Surely the police would be along at daybreak to discover us, and there was no human way that we could change our situation. We knew that we needed a miracle.

So, standing together with our hands joined in agreement, we thanked the Lord for the transmission that He was going to install. Then we climbed back into the truck. Roberto started the engine, and we drove away. In the mirror, I could see the old transmission still lying on the road. For the next four hours of travel, our hearts were full of songs and praise to our Lord for this wonderful miracle!

At 7:00 A.M., we arrived at the house of Martin, another Cuban brother who would join us in our "journey for Jesus." When Martin saw us arrive, he came out of his house, and with a surprised look, exclaimed, "Where did you get that truck? I saw it in my dream last night."

We said nothing as he continued. "I saw that very truck coming east along the highway. You three were in the front. Roberto was driving."

We just stood and listened in amazement.

"Then," added Martin, "I saw a dark figure following over the top of the truck. Part of that figure went under the truck and touched your transmission and it fell to the ground! I jumped to my feet, and shouted, 'I saw you do that, satan! You put that back right now!' Then I saw you start again down the highway, but the transmission was still on the ground. Now why would I have a dream like that?"

"Because that is exactly what happened," Roberto told him. Martin was astonished and amazed.

"Martin, did you notice what time you had that dream?" I asked.

"Yes," he replied. "I looked at the clock. It was 3:00 A.M."

"That is the very time that this all happened," I said. We all then knelt down to thank our Father for this wonderful miracle of His love.

This was the beginning of a marvelous two-week journey together in search of souls for Jesus, and how good He was to us, in every place, protecting us, giving an abundance of His Spirit and His joy as we reached many hungry souls with His Word as well as His healing and delivering power. There is great joy in serving Jesus!

Let me add this final word of praise to our Lord. While we remained in that town, Marcos visited a friend who was a mechanic and asked him to come and check the transmission. In the meantime, Roberto parked the truck on the grass so that it would be easy to crawl under. When the mechanic arrived, he slid under the truck, came back out, brushed the grass off himself, and said, "I don't know what you are all worried about. Someone has installed a new transmission in this thing!" You can imagine what our conversation was about the rest of that day and evening!

The next day, we began our journey to other towns and villages, and the truck continued to run smoothly with no transmission problems. At one point, I heard Roberto, while driving, comment, "It sure would have been nice of the Lord if He had fixed this sloppy steering wheel."

"But we didn't ask Him for that," replied Marcos.

How good it was to have been with my Cuban brothers, through whom I learned so much! Thank You, Lord, for all You add to my life through Your children all over the world.

THE NAME OF JESUS

It is a marvelous comfort to remember the words of our Lord, "All that the Father giveth Me shall come to Me; and him that cometh to Me I will in no wise cast out" (John 6:37). "And I give unto them eternal life; and they shall never perish, neither shall any man pluck them out of My hand" (John 10:28). As we travel from place to place, we recognize that there are chosen ones whom the Lord foreknew before the foundation of the world, and He has provided the means to call them through the Word of God, the Holy Spirit, and the name of Jesus. There are those who preach the Word, and have somehow thought that the name of Jesus is to be proclaimed only through the message that is preached. Yet He is waiting for our hands to be laid upon the sick, so that they can recover, in the powerful name of Jesus, even as Peter and John did when they spoke to the lame man at the gate of the temple, as found in Acts 3:6-8:

> *Then Peter said...In the name of Jesus Christ of Nazareth rise up and walk. And he took him by the right hand, and lifted him up: and immediately his feet and ankle bones received strength. And he leaping up stood, and walked, and entered with them into the temple, walking, and leaping, and praising God.*

This miracle would bring over five thousand people into the family of God.

Those who refused to believe in that name were the religious people. And what did they do? They took hold of Peter and John, and threw them into jail. The next day, they brought them out to stand next to the man who was healed, and asked them, "By what power, or by what name, have ye done this?" (Acts 4:7b). Peter answered them, being filled with the Holy Spirit,

> *Be it known unto you all, and to all the people of Israel, that by the name of Jesus Christ of Nazareth, whom ye crucified, whom God raised from the dead, even by Him doth this man stand here before you whole. This is the stone which was set at nought of you builders, which is become the head of the corner. Neither is there salvation*

in any other: for there is none other name under heaven given among men, whereby we must be saved (Acts 4:10-12).

"The stone which was set at nought!" That is the name of Jesus. And He is set at nought today, also. Although the disciples admired the structure of the temple, Jesus said that it would all soon come down. Moreover, while there are many church buildings all over the earth today, still He does not live in any of them.

JESUS SAYS, "COME," "FOLLOW ME," AND "GO"

Jesus was from Nazareth, but could perform very few miracles there because they had already categorized Him as "the carpenter's son."

Here is a word to you carpenters: Jesus is ready to use your hands, too, to do His miracles, as you preach His Word. Souls everywhere will come to Him. Here is a word to you fishermen: Jesus says, "Follow Me, and I will make you fishers of men" (Matt. 4:19). Step out of the boat, as Peter did. Yes, his faith was a little on the crazy side, but surely a crazy faith is better than a commercial faith. While the others chose to stay in the shaky boat, the Lord said to Peter, "Come." Yet He didn't calm the sea to quiet his nerves. Jesus said, "Lo, I am with you always, even unto the end of the world" (Matt. 28:20b). Yes, Peter did sink after a few steps of success, and we may also. But Jesus is there to pull us up. He will always pull us up when we call for help. However, you may choose to stay with the majority, tossed around in the little boat, yet you still are not exempt from danger. It is better to walk with Jesus wherever He goes.

Have you heard Jesus say, "Come"? Then get out of the boat. The only safe place and the only place where we will receive the constant flow of His blessings, is with Him. And if we start to sink, He will tell us why.

Our Lord has also said, "Go"—a powerful word that requires obedience. It doesn't necessarily mean "move," although it may include that. What are you doing for Him now? Do you *go* to your neighbors? Do you *go* to your family? Do you *go* to the hospitals and prisons? "Go," says our Lord. And unless you obey Him, you will never know the ultimate blessings our Lord has waiting for you. If you hear His command, but do nothing, you are like the slothful servant who did nothing with his one talent, and in the end, he lost it as well (see Matt. 25:14-30).

We need, also, to put our children on the altar of the Lord, and leave them there, allowing Him to lead them wherever He directs them to go. They are His inheritance. To do anything otherwise is to make them idols unto ourselves. If we love the Lord our God with all our heart, all our soul, and all our strength, then we love Him first of all. And if we love Him first of all, we cannot love our children first of all. The fact is our children receive more love from us when we love Jesus first and most. It is the same with our spouses. The love between spouses is always stronger when they each love Jesus first and foremost.

LOVE IS OBEDIENCE

What does our Savior desire most from us? What did He create us for? Listen to His own words coming straight from His heart. "He that hath My commandments, and keepeth them, he it is that loveth Me: and he that loveth Me shall be loved of My Father, and I will love him, and will manifest Myself to him" (John 14:21).

The proof of our love is not our words to Him, but rather our obedience to Him. For some believers, His commands are simply words written on the pages of the Bible. For others, His commands are a part of their minds and memories. And there is yet another group who puts them into practice. Three groups of believers:

1. Those who know there are commandments.

2. Those who, little by little, are becoming acquainted with the commandments.

3. Those who obey the commandments.

In John chapter 14, Jesus was referring to those who not only know the commandments, but also obey them. Thus, they love Him and will see Him manifest Himself in their lives.

Let's also notice an added blessing in verse 23: "If a man love Me, he will keep My words: and My Father will love him, and We will come unto him, and make Our abode with him" (John 14:23). Now we see something more wonderful still. Here, He says that not only will He come and be with us, manifesting Himself to us, but that His Father will also participate in that love that we show to Jesus by obeying His commands. And He shares a secret, something very special: "My Father will love him, and We will come unto him and make Our abode with him." What a marvelous truth this is! We already have the Holy Spirit living within; then come the Father and the Son to make their loving abode with us here and now. We have the Trinity! We can have them all the time, as long as we show Him our love through our obedience. This is Heaven on earth. This is the environment in which Jesus does His miracles. It is through this love relationship that He can do the "greater things" of which He spoke (see John 14:12).

It was David who said, "Search me, O God, and know my heart…" (Ps. 139:23); and "bless the Lord, O my soul: and all that is within me, bless His holy name" (Ps. 103:1). It was David who also said, "One thing have I desired of the Lord, that will I seek after; that I may dwell in the house of the Lord all the days of my life, to behold the beauty of the Lord, and to enquire in His temple" (Ps. 27:4).

Today we do not have to inquire in His temple. Rather, He has promised His dwelling place will be with us continually in exchange for our love and obedience. It was because of David's love for Him, that our Lord said, "I have found David, the son of Jesse, a man after mine own heart, which shall fulfill all my will." (Acts 13:22). Does this sound like God has favorites? How do we do interpret the expression in the Bible, "Jacob have I loved, but Esau have I hated" (Rom. 9:13)? By the way, the word *hate* in the original means "love less than." Esau could have received the love, but he did not reciprocate what love he had been given. So then, it still all comes down to what Jesus said, "If ye love Me, keep My commandments" (John 14:15). John, the "disciple whom Jesus loved" echoes this in his Epistle of First John: "For this is the love of God, that we keep His commandments: and His commandments are not grievous" (1 John 5:3). John walked in the presence of the Lord Jesus, and of the Father, and even in this short epistle, he mentions the love of God 44 times.

Try as we may, if we have not experienced death to ourselves, we will not experience His loving presence with us, and His power through us. God is love, and He, being love, will consume us with His love, the essence of His person and His power.

Chapter Eleven

OUT OF THE
MOUTHS OF BABES

⚓

People who hear about our encounters with the forces of darkness sometimes ask us if we allow our children to be present in those times of deliverance. For the most part, yes. The Lord has revealed these things unto babes. When they learn together with us through the years, it becomes second nature for them to take authority over demonic spirits, and to cast them out. It matters not their size or their age; there is great authority in the name of Jesus.

CHILDLIKE FAITH

Many years ago, in Guatemala, a deacon of the church said to me one day, "Brother Levi, my daughter has had epilepsy for the last ten years, since she was six years old. Could you come to my house and pray for her?"

"Will be glad to," I answered. "Only let's take two days first to fast and pray for her."

So we did. And on the appointed day, I took our two youngest boys, Ruben and Shalom, ages 9 and 7, with me. As we sat talking to this brother, he called his 16-year-old daughter into the living room, and presented her. He was surprised when I told him that my sons were going to pray for her.

"Are they qualified for this?" he asked, slightly nervous.

"Only the name of Jesus is qualified," I answered.

Informing the devil that his time was up, they laid hands on her, and commanded the epileptic spirit to come up and get out, in the name of Jesus. Immediately, the spirit began to stir, shaking and convulsing her. The boys were not bothered, but insisted, "Out with you! In Jesus' name!" And out it came, never to return. I simply watched.

Dear reader, why am I relating this to you? Because the most important thing for us to understand is the power and authority that are in the name of Jesus. For "out of the mouth of babes…[He has] ordained strength" (Ps. 8:2a). We, as adults, cannot enter into the Kingdom of Heaven unless we enter as babes. A child believes what he is told, until he learns from adults the practice of doubting most anything.

It is such a delight to go to places on this earth where there are people with a childlike faith. These places are where we've acquired much learning. Unfortunately, in the Western world, there is a problem with head knowledge. I am not despising education, for it is very necessary. However, it also poses a problem, which Paul speaks about—"knowledge puffeth up…" (1 Cor. 8:1b). We need to understand this reality, and come to our Lord for the humbling process. It is not easy to do, for to humble ourselves under the mighty hand of God means to "re-die" every day. We were born with our head over our heart, but now we need to allow Him to move our heart over our head.

INHERITED SPIRITS

Many years ago, in southern Mexico, I met a young man named Juanito, who was studying in a Bible school to become a pastor. Juanito, because of his deep love for our Lord, was a very likeable young man. One day he invited me to his home in the country where he lived with his parents in the Huave Indian zone, along the coast of Oaxaca. The Huaves are said to have come from Peru on a ship several centuries ago, having suffered shipwreck along that southern Mexican coast. They came ashore and established themselves there, predominantly as fishermen. They are a humble, sincere people, most of them very friendly.

As Juanito and I visited in his home where he lived with his parents, I noticed that his abdomen was making convulsive waves, and causing him great distress.

"There is something moving around on the inside of me that doesn't like your presence," he said. "It speaks to me, and says that I belong to lucifer, and I'm assigned to serve him all my life. It tells me to beware of you, that you are going to harm me." Just then, Juanito cried out, "No, you are the false one, satan. I don't want you inside of me. I only want Jesus!" As I laid a hand on Juanito, the spirits began to come forth, in Jesus' name, leaving him at peace.

We then sat down, and Juanito explained to me that his father was a *curandero* that is, a witch doctor, and daily practiced witchcraft. For many of you who are reading this, what I have just stated might be difficult to understand. But continue reading, and I believe you will comprehend it.

Soon thereafter, Juanito finished Bible school and was given a small church to pastor. Even though I had spent time with him at the home of his parents, I still did not realize how deep the problem of witchcraft was within his own body and soul areas. He prayed often, but found that this was like stirring up a hornets' nest, which likewise happened when he read or studied the Bible. Within his spirit, he felt a deep love for Jesus, but when he tried to tell the Lord how much he loved Him, he would curl up with abdominal pain.

But the strangest things took place while he was preaching. The more he felt the Spirit's anointing, the greater the demonic powers within opposed him. One day in the middle of his preaching, the evil spirits threw him on the floor. There he writhed in pain, and finally struggled to get up. When this happened during several meetings, the church, not understanding the nature of what was happening, judged Juanito wrongly, and accused him of living a life of secret sin.

When he came to me, he was deeply hurt, understandably, knowing that he was not doing the things of which he was accused. He had been expelled from the pastorate and condemned before all in that little town, yet no one could bring any specific charges against him. It was a crisis time of discouragement for him, and I felt led to invite him to come to our home in Guatemala. And he agreed.

Juanito spent the next eight months with us in Guatemala. Daily we prayed over him, often fasting for him, and daily there were more and more spirits coming out of him, often with screams or convulsions, and always with pain. When I had to be away for other commitments, our sons would take turns helping in his deliverance. It seemed as though we would never come to the end of it. Toward the end of the seventh month, however, we noticed that the manifestations were occurring less and less. Then in the middle of the eighth month, they completely stopped. Juanito could pray now in the Spirit, unhindered, and he could preach with the anointing without being thrown on the floor.

We then returned to Mexico and to his home. Although he had never participated in the witchcraft which his father practiced, he had been affected by the spirits. Whereas his father had never experienced any of the manifestations that he had, the reason being that his father was not a believer in Christ. It is when the Holy Spirit comes to live within our spirit that the evil spirits in the realm of the soul and the body become disquieted and uncomfortable.

Back at home, Juanito was now 27, and experienced a new inner peace that he had never known before. Soon, he found himself a good Christian wife, and today, many years later, they serve the Lord, pastoring a growing church, together with their children. Each of them knows satan's tactics, and how to set people free from the power of satan.

Jesus has told us to tread upon serpents, not literal snakes, but the spirit serpents that we find so often imbedded in people. Many times these serpents throw a person to the floor, causing him or her to writhe all over the room like a serpent, and even hissing with the tongue extended. This has been a common happening, and some of you who read this might have seen this in person. We praise our Lord again for His grace, for the power of Jesus' name, for the enabling of His Holy Spirit, and for the privilege of seeing the captives set free. Yet we know that this authority is not the source of our rejoicing, but rather all that our Lord has done for us, and for writing our names in His Book of Life in Heaven. What we do does not make us worthy, for He alone is worthy to receive the honor and glory. As you read on, remember always to turn your eyes on our glorious Lord Jesus, who teaches us, "Herein is My Father glorified, that ye bear much fruit; so shall ye be My disciples" (John 15:8).

Chapter Twelve

THE DEVIL THROWS ROCKS

⚓

The following account was one of the most unusual happenings that we have ever witnessed. It reveals how God and satan work often at the same time. Of course, God always comes out the winner; and in the end, God will use whatever satan does to fulfill His own purposes and bring glory to His own name. As a family, we have come to the conclusion that the devil is the Lord's "pick and shovel" man, meaning he must carry the pick and shovel for the Lord, and dig all His ditches. Then when he gets those done, the Lord says to him, "Now turn those ditches over to Me." Is this not what happened in the case of Job?

It was October 1990, and we were living in Guatemala on the eastern side. One Friday afternoon, upon returning home from a preaching trip, my wife, Lily, set a cup of tea before me and handed me the newspaper. I opened it to find nearly the entire paper full of pictures of the same news story. I am not one to disbelieve the supernatural, but this beat anything I had ever heard.

The family of Israel Palma, including his wife, Lola, and five children, were all sound asleep in their little adobe house nestled in the hills of eastern Guatemala. It was around 11:00 P.M., and raining outside when the sound of a rock, landing on their roof and then rolling off, woke Israel from a sound sleep. This is sometimes the way a neighbor will call another at night. Israel got up and stood before the closed door, and spoke loudly, "Who is it?" There was no answer. He tried again. Still no answer. So he returned to his bed, and went back to sleep.

A short while later, another rock fell on the roof and stayed there. Israel jumped from bed again and stood before the door. "Who is it?" he bellowed. There was no answer. Again, he returned to bed. Unable to sleep, he listened to the rain falling on the roof tiles above; and before long, another rock hit the roof, this one so big that it broke the tiles and landed next to their bed, allowing the rain to pour in. Israel was perplexed, especially because their house was not near any mountain where rocks could tumble down.

Somebody is trying to kill us, he thought, and reached for his gun. As he stood again before the closed door, he shouted, "Who is it?" once, twice, three times. Still there was no answer. Israel then fired a bullet through the door, and immediately the gun was jerked from his hand by an invisible force and could be found nowhere in the room! The only thing left to do was to go back to bed and wait for the dawn. The rocks continued to pellet the roof during the night, as the rain came in next to the bed.

Around 6:00 A.M. the family was up and about, surveying the damage. Many tiles had been broken, and they had no money with which to replace them. Israel went up on the roof to pull down the rocks that hadn't rolled down, and remove the broken tiles, while Lola went to the neighbors to inform them of what had happened. They all came and stood, gazing at the damage in utter disbelief. Soon they each went to their houses and came back with an armload of tiles to help with the repairs.

It didn't take long for Israel and his sons to put the tiles in place, and then he set out to work in his cornfield. Hoeing between the corn and meditating on the events of the night, he heard the sounds of rocks moving, and turned around to find a large rock lifting itself off the ground by an invisible force. As soon as he looked at it, however, the rock went back down to the ground. He continued his work. Again and again he watched the rock rise and watched it go back down. Finally, when he wasn't paying attention, the rock was hurled at him with force, hitting him in the middle of the back, leaving him with a painful bruise, and unable to continue his work. Israel hobbled home, where his wife bathed and dressed his wound.

The word spread around town, and once again the neighbors all came to see what had happened to their dear neighbor, Israel, and looked at each other in disbelief. Again, during the next night more rocks fell on their house, some of them so big that a strong man could not lift them, let alone hurl them.

In the morning, other neighbors brought additional roof tiles, and one of them volunteered his help. "Israel," he said, "while your boys are putting on those tiles, I'll go with you to the corn field and look out for you as you work."

So it was. Israel went amongst his corn, and resumed his work hoeing the weeds, while his neighbor sat on a big rock in the clearing. Everything seemed to go fine for a while, but soon Israel thought he heard some rocks falling, and made his way out of the rows of corn. There he saw a pile of rocks that hadn't been there before, but his neighbor was nowhere in sight. So Israel shouted his name as loud as he could, while standing next to the rock pile. He then thought he heard a groan that was coming from under the pile of rocks. He tried to lift them off each other, but most of the rocks were too big, so he ran to get some neighbors to help. Together they lifted the boulders and found his neighbor badly wounded. He was taken to the hospital in Jalapa, two hours away on rugged roads, and there he stayed for several weeks. This was a painful event for Israel and Lola, knowing that this neighbor had almost lost his life for their sake.

The stones continued to bombard the Palma house every few days, and they changed the roof tiles six times. During this time, different priests from around the country came, bringing idols, candles, crosses, red ribbons, and sprinkling their holy water. Nothing availed. Obviously, there was a satanic plot employing demonic activity to kill the Palma family. Finally, Israel's sister, Vilda, walked from her town, San Pedro Pinula, to Israel's home.

"Look, Israel," she said, "obviously your house has a curse on it. You had better bring your things, you and the family, and come to live with me in Pinula."

So they decided that was the only thing left to do. They gathered a few things together, and walked the two kilometers to Vilda's house.

However, it wasn't long after settling in with Vilda that the rocks arrived again, coming through the open center patio and into Vilda's house, breaking the windows, and destroying everything in sight, including the television screen, the wardrobe, lamps, and eyeglasses left on a table. By now, the press from many countries was getting wind of these events, and reporters were showing up from everywhere. Some of them were pelted by stones, as they described, "thrown by an invisible force."

Also during this time, the archbishop of Guatemala City (five hours away) was asked to do something about it, with his "most holy water." After his short visit, the archbishop made a exit and hurried back to Guatemala City. Later, when asked by the press to comment, he said only that there must be some scientific explanation for it. Needless to say, the problem continued.

When I read all this information in the newspaper, I commented to my wife that this was one matter that I would not be getting involved in, and with that, I decided to retire early for the night, being tired from my journeys.

That same evening, our son, Alfred, was with some friends in town, who commented about the events with the stones in Agua Zarca and Pinula, two hours away.

"Do you think your father will go over there to do something for those people?" they asked him.

"Oh, yes! You can be sure he'll be there!" he affirmed. But those were not my intentions.

That night, I slept from nine until eleven, and awoke suddenly. Not knowing why, I asked the Lord, *Is that You, Lord?* He answered within my spirit, *Yes. Did you say you will have nothing to do with going to the family who is being attacked by the stones? Yes, Lord,* I replied. *Will you go, if I send you?* the Lord asked. *Yes, Lord, but I ask You to give me a definite sign that You are in this.* With that, I went back to sleep.

At seven the next morning on a Friday, during breakfast, my wife asked me if I would walk with her to the marketplace. It is not my favorite thing to do, but I wanted to be with her. So, we went to the banana stand. Lily had gotten to know several of these merchants who were Christians, and the banana lady, Leila, introduced us to a fellow believer, named Irma, across the aisle. Irma came across to meet us, and during our conversation she began to relate something urgent.

"I have a sister, named Lola," she said. "She and her husband, Israel, and their five children, live in a village about two hours from here, called Agua Zarca. Something terrible has been happening! The devil has been trying to kill them with rocks! Several people have gone there to help them, and have been stoned and bruised. Do you think you can go and help?"

"Why, yes, I believe so," I answered.

My wife looked at me and said, "Really?"

"Yes," I replied, "and you're going with me."

I knew she'd be in agreement, because she's nearly as crazy as I am. We both recognized this encounter as from the Lord, so we decided to go on Monday, first using the weekend for prayer and fasting. Meanwhile, Irma sent a messenger to Vilda's house in Pinula, saying that we would arrive there at 10:00 A.M. on Monday. We both felt peaceful about whatever was to take place because the Lord had given this miraculous confirmation at the market. Who would ever guess that we would find a family member in a marketplace at such a distance from the scene, and that she would immediately ask for our help? This is what I had asked the Lord for.

On Monday at 8:00 A.M., we found ourselves on the rough road to Pinula, where the Palma family was residing with Israel's sister, Vilda. Arriving near their house at 10:00 A.M., we stopped the van and observed the rocks all about the front. We took time for special prayer for His protection, and also made a prophetic statement aloud, saying, "There will be no more rocks ever move again against the Palma family, against this house, or against their house." With that, we felt a peace, and got out of the van. Not a stone moved.

We were greeted warmly at the door and were asked to come in and sit down. Destruction was everywhere, resembling the aftermath of a tornado. Israel went over all the history of the past few weeks, which was like reading it again, only with much more detail. Then he pointed to a small fluorescent light in the ceiling.

"You see that 20-watt tube lamp above? I'll tell you what happened—why it's broken. You see, there was a professor in town who was telling people that this was all false, and he would prove it. So he came to the house. He must have thought that we had created the scene ourselves. Being inside the house, he was caught unawares by a large stone that lifted up and hit him in the left leg below the knee. The pain was so strong that he sat down to rub it. Then he lifted that heavy rock onto a chair, and told it, 'Now, you stay right there!' Imagine! And he didn't believe in any of this! Before he was able to leave, the rock shot off that chair and hit that fluorescent light, breaking the tube into little pieces before his eyes. He hobbled to the door and limped home. We never heard another word from him."

Meanwhile, the Lord was helping us to guide the conversation into spiritual matters, and this is what they wanted. We showed them that Jesus not only came to save them, but also to destroy the works of the devil (see 1 John 3:8). Soon they were opening their hearts to our Savior, and the whole family came into His fold.

After having lunch with the Palmas, we asked if they would like to return to their house in Agua Zarca. They were in agreement, and soon got their few possessions together. We escorted them into our five-seater van, and started the two-kilometer drive to Agua Zarca. After crossing a little river, we arrived at their house (perhaps better stated, what was left of it). Piles of rocks, large and small, were everywhere. On the inside were gaping holes in most of the roof. Their bed was covered with a large piece of plastic, with a puddle of rain water on it.

We started gathering all the idols, candles, red ribbons, and all other items that were supposed to have gotten rid of the problem, took them out, and destroyed them. Next, we joined our hands in agreement, and thanking the Lord for the victory, we also audibly spoke to satan and his forces that they would never be allowed on this property again, or to attack their home or the persons therein in any manner.

Then Israel, a man in his 60's, spoke, "We are so grateful!"

"Israel," I said, "we are not finished. God willing, we will return on Wednesday with more roof tiles, and our sons will put them on so that no more rain will come in."

"Thank you so much," he replied, "but I also should say that we have changed that roof six times, and there are no more roof tiles to be found in any of the towns within two hours."

"Well, if I have to, I will travel to Guatemala City for them," I assured him.

As we drove away to return to our home in Jalapa, we felt the peace of God everywhere, and knew that this satanic attack would never happen again. Indeed, it never has.

The next day I went looking everywhere for roof tiles. He was right. There were none to be found. Then toward evening, when I was about to quit, someone told me that he saw smoke coming out of a brick furnace over behind the hills. I found the road to reach the place, and sure enough, they had decided to bake roof tiles.

"Are those tiles ready to sell?" I asked.

"Yes. How many do you want?" he responded.

Strange that I had not even calculated the amount. I said, "I don't know. Let me ask the Lord."

The man must have been a Christian. "For sure," he commented.

The Lord gave me a number. "One hundred sixty-three," I told him.

"That's a strange number," he remarked, "but one hundred sixty-three it will be." I watched as he stacked them carefully into the van, and then paid him.

Back at the house, Lily was getting things ready for our journey back to Agua Zarca the next day. I informed the boys of what their job would be, and they were delighted. To my son, Andre, I gave a special message.

"Andre," I said, "the Palma family has a son, Edgar, who is 16. He has a great desire to learn the guitar, to serve the Lord. I promised him that I would give him this beautiful guitar if he would learn to play it within 30 days. If you spend the day tomorrow, teaching him, then you are exempt from helping to put on the roof tiles." He liked this idea, and fulfilled his part of the agreement.

It was a glorious day, and while the roof was being installed, we had sweet fellowship with the Palmas, and taught them some Christian choruses. The boys did a good job on the roof, using up every one of the tiles. There were none too few, and none too many. That left still a little time to roll some stones out of the way, as there were many that were too big to lift.

Before leaving, we gathered for prayer, and I informed Edgar that we would be back in 30 days to see how he was doing on the guitar, and to hold a meeting, inviting all the people of the village. He knew that he would have to work hard to be able to play in 30 days; then that beautiful guitar would be his.

And work hard, he did! When we returned in 30 days, he was playing the guitar quite well! And when we announced that it was now his, tears came to his eyes as he handed it to me, saying, "Please dedicate it to the Lord." So we dedicated both him and the guitar.

The boys unloaded our equipment—an electric generator (there was no electricity in that town), a film projector, and a 60-minute film. We stretched a large white sheet and tied it between two trees, to work as a screen. The image thus could be seen on both sides.

Israel and I then went house to house to invite the whole village. Over 200 people showed up at the appropriate time. Following the movie and the message, I asked how many would like to ask Jesus to be their Savior. Every hand went up. Wondering if they understood, I repeated the question with more clarity. Again, every hand went up. So we prayed together, and each one made a decision to invite the Lord Jesus to be his or her Savior.

Talking with several people later, I discovered that it was not the film, nor the message, but rather the miracle of what God had done for the Palma family that convinced them of their need for the Lord Jesus as their Savior. So...once again, the devil had to dig the ditches, and turn them all over to Him.

Chapter Thirteen

A RARE TREASURE IN THE RIGHT PLACE AT THE RIGHT TIME

⚓

Yes, we have seen it again and again…a crisis that turns into a miracle! And so it was with our 1972 Dodge van. It had been a faithful vehicle, enabling us to travel to places that were difficult to reach.

One day, in Guatemala City, I stopped by to see our Christian mechanic. He looked over the van, and said, "It's in good shape, Brother Levi, but if I were you, the next time I was in the U.S., I would sell it and get another vehicle. If that transmission goes out, you will not find a replacement for it anywhere in Guatemala."

I took his advice to heart and tucked the information in the back of my mind; however there were no plans for a trip to the U.S. anytime soon. Well, you can guess what happened. Yes, one day, as I was traveling away from civilization, and just before entering a small village, the transmission stopped functioning, and I recalled the mechanic's words. Even so, I left the vehicle and went walking the dusty road in search of some kind of help. Along the way, I saw an elderly man with a cane.

"Sir, do you know if there is a mechanic's shop in this town?" I asked.

"Why, sure, there is," he answered. "It's right down the road on the other side."

I looked hard, but I couldn't see it.

"You see that tree with the chain and hook hanging from it? That's the mechanic's shop."

As I approached the tree, I saw a grease spot on the ground under the chain. Then I saw a house on the hill behind the tree, and I continued walking. Upon seeing the grease around the door knob, I assumed it was the mechanic's house.

I knocked on the door, and the mechanic opened it. It was 8:00 A.M., and he was having breakfast. After I was invited in, I found myself sitting at his table with some coffee and sweet-bread set before me.

"What can I help you with?" he asked across the table.

I began to explain what happened to my van's transmission.

"What year did you say?" he asked.

"'72 Dodge van," I repeated.

"Transmission?"

"Yes, sir."

"You've got a problem," he said. "There aren't any!"

Great comfort he was!

"But you see that thing over there in the corner of the room?" It was leaking oil all over the floor. "It's been sitting there for two years, and my wife said that I'd better get it out of here before she divorces me. You came to save my marriage!" he said, laughing.

"Why's that?" I asked.

"Because that's the very transmission you need!"

I thought I was going to fall over! "No kidding! How did it get to this little town?" I questioned.

"Well, two years ago, an American with that same model of van drove through this town, and his engine burned up right in front of my house. The only thing that was still good was the transmission. He gave it to me and junked the rest. So it has been sitting in here away from the rain, waiting for you."

We both sat, still at the table, amazed at the way God had synchronized our circumstances. We settled on a very reasonable price, and it was to be ready in three days.

At the appointed time, I returned to the tree with the chain and the mechanic on the hill. Once again, we sat together for breakfast. I felt in my spirit that God had chosen this family for salvation, and continued to share with them from the Word of the Lord. Within a short while, they all opened their hearts to the Lord, and indeed, there was great rejoicing in Heaven and on earth that day. These are the works of the Lord, and marvelous in our eyes.

During my conversation with the mechanic and his family, I realized that what had convinced them the most to open their hearts to God's mercy, was the way He led me to the only place in the country where a transmission so rare could be found.

Chapter Fourteen

ANOTHER PIECE OF THE PUZZLE

It was September 2000 when I found myself in the suburbs of Boston. A Hispanic church pastor had asked me if I would speak to his congregation on Sunday evening. I replied that I had already made one commitment to speak on that day at 8:00 P.M. at another church. Then he asked if I would come at 6:00 P.M. My answer was yes, as long as I could leave promptly at 7:45 P.M. That was fine.

The day came, and knowing that it was going to be a long one, I asked the Lord for strength, and a special anointing, which sometimes ebbs when we are tired. As I spoke to the 6:00 P.M. group, I looked out over the crowd and saw a young man who not only paid close attention, but looked like he was about to jump out of his seat.

When the message was over, I explained that even though I would like to continue to minister and visit with them, I had to go to another meeting. Seeing that they understood, I proceeded rather hurriedly out the front door. As I started across the street to where my car was parked, I heard someone calling from behind me. Turning around on the sidewalk, I saw the same young man who had listened so intently. He suddenly embraced me with tears in his eyes.

"Don't you remember me, Brother Levi? I'm Edgar, from Agua Zarca."

"The Lord bless you. Yes, you are! How did you get to Boston?" I asked.

"I came up to work and earn enough money to build a tortilla factory on our property. We now have electricity in our village." He replied.

"And do you still play the guitar?"

"More than ever, and I am the youth pastor at our church. We now have a church building, and all those people who received Jesus that night come to it!"

I tried to clear my eyes of the tears that were coming up from the surge of joy in my heart.

"Lord, this is for real!" I cried.

Edgar hugged me again, and said, "I know you must hurry. My parents and family are all fine. I am married, and we have a two-year-old daughter. Nobody is going to believe where we met!" he shouted as he started across the street.

It seemed almost like a dream, as I watched him disappear back into the church. Getting into the car, I had to sit a few minutes to dry my eyes before driving. I don't know if there are any words to describe the joy that comes to us as we serve Jesus.

Chapter Fifteen

WHATSOEVER YE SHALL ASK

⚓

Just before going to the cross, our Lord spoke of the joy that He experienced. "These things have I spoken unto you, that My joy might remain in you, and that your joy might be full" (John 15:11). He wants us to have not just a *little* joy, or *some* joy, but *fullness* of joy. Furthermore, He tells us how to have it: "Hitherto have ye asked nothing in My name: ask, and ye shall receive, that your joy may be full" (John 16:24).

Of course, we can ask for whatever we need, and He is delighted to give it to us when we are walking with Him. However, there are things eternal, which the Holy Spirit places on our hearts, so that we might ask for them. These include changes within us that He wants to bring about—that *internal fruit* that is His own character: love, joy, peace, longsuffering, gentleness, goodness, faith, meekness, temperance (see Gal. 5:22-23). We are also to ask for that *external fruit* that adds to His Kingdom—souls to be brought to Him, edifying of the saints, healing of the sick, binding the "strongman" wherever he is found, and encouraging the afflicted. These are the petitions that we set before the Lord, and He is pleased to give them to us. Consequently, there is a fountain of joy produced within us. He wants His joy to *remain* in us, and He wants us to have it continuously.

On the other hand, the enemy wants to steal this joy, for he is a thief. Once he steals your joy, you will become depressed. And if you don't recognize what has happened, you might mistakenly think that buying some joke books or taking some pills will help solve your problems. Nevertheless, ask Him where you have gone astray, confess your faults, and return to the joy of abiding in Jesus.

Then increase that joy by asking for whatever you need, and by requesting eternal fruit.

"Seek ye first the kingdom of God, and His righteousness; and all these things shall be added unto you" (Matt. 6:33). "In Thy [His] presence is fullness of joy; at Thy [His] right hand there are pleasures for evermore" (Ps. 16:11b). Obey His command; go to the lost and needy. You then will realize not only His presence that He has promised, but also the joy that goes with it.

Chapter Sixteen

WHITE CASTLE

Many years ago, God gave us a vision of building a retreat in southern Mexico where pastors could come and learn, pray, and fellowship together. As we prayed, He led us to a parcel of land, about ten acres, in the isthmus area of the state of Oaxaca, nestled between the hills and mountains at an elevation where the climate was ideal year round.

The land, surprisingly, was not expensive; however, we still waited several years to build because of lack of funding. The Lord had put His own plans into our thoughts as to the structure and design, yet we had not started.

Soon, though, we understood that we should not wait any longer, but should begin clearing away the jungle. It was one thing to cut down the trees, but it was another to dig out the trunks and roots. This went on for weeks. Finally, we were able to put stakes on all the corners of what would become *Beth Shalom*. This was not to be any small structure. Digging for the foundations started, even while we still had no money for the concrete and steel. So we prayed as we continued to labor. And by the time the digging was finished, enough money had been received in order to pour the concrete.

Having done that, we then had little money to continue the structure. I stood back one day, gazing at the site of our future building, and the Lord said, *Take what money you have left, and buy some fruit trees to plant all around the place.* As this thought came to my mind, I remembered where there was a nursery, and started out in our pickup. As I turned off the highway into the nursery, a very clear message came from the Holy Spirit into my thoughts, saying, *I have chosen this entire family who runs this nursery. Be diligent to bring them to Me.* This set me to thinking and praying, as I introduced myself to the proprietor, Luis, his wife, Maria, his son, Luis, and their five other children.

As we chose the fruit trees—mangos, bananas, grapefruit, oranges, lemons, papayas—we engaged in a conversation that soon led to spiritual matters. Before leaving with the trees, I reached into the cab of my truck for a New Testament with extra large print, and handed it to the father, saying, "This is a part of the Bible. I know that you will enjoy reading it. It tells of the life of Jesus, how He died for us, and how to have eternal life."

Luis reached out his hands to receive the Bible, and expressing thanks, pressed it to his bosom, saying, "We will read it as a family."

We kept the family in our prayers, and one month later, when Lily and I returned to the nursery for more plants, we found that they had read the whole New Testament aloud, and were deeply stirred with what they had understood. We sat down under the shade of a tree to answer their questions, and then around a picnic table to have lunch together. It was evident that God's Spirit was working in each heart.

A few days later, we returned for more plants. On this occasion, we were told that the oldest daughter, also named Maria, was found to have tuberculosis, and we asked if we could pray for her. Lily and I laid hands on her, giving thanks to the Lord for healing, and began to command the tuberculosis to come out of her. She immediately began to cough excessively, and then suddenly the coughing was gone.

"It's gone!" she said. "I feel fine. I can breathe easily." After that moment, the tuberculosis never returned, and the following tuberculosis tests were negative. This was the turning point for the family, and there, around the picnic table, all of them gave their hearts to Jesus.

Since that day, this family has grown rapidly in the Lord, and has preached the Gospel in many places, formed missions, and encouraged the brethren. When Luis felt the call of God, he sold the nursery, and today works full-time as a pastor. He takes good care of God's flock and is seeing many others come to Jesus. What a joy to see the Lord fulfilling His promises to us! Yes, He does save souls today. And He also heals bodies for His glory. Luis and his family continue to do the works that Jesus did, bringing souls to the Savior by preaching the Word, healing the sick, and casting out demonic spirits.

The construction of the white castle, *Beth Shalom*, continued, and with the ground floor almost finished in 1997, we moved from Guatemala, where we had lived for eight years, to Mexico to occupy the building. Today, the retreat is four stories high. From its prayer towers are unusual views of the mountains for hundreds of miles. The 15,000 square-foot building, all made of concrete and steel, can accommodate sizeable groups for pastors and for youth groups. Throughout the entire process of building, none of the construction ever needed to be financed, for the Lord had instructed us to pray in the funds by faith.

The youth groups continue to be large, usually about 150 in number, coming from several states, and have been spiritually fruitful and multiplying in many places. It is a work of faith, and we depend entirely on the Lord for resources of food for such large groups, and for maintenance. Each time, we see Him faithfully fulfill His promise, "I will never leave you nor forsake you" (Josh. 1:5b NIV).

Chapter Seventeen

SATAN'S VENGEANCE

⚓

A HEART IS HEALED

In December 2004, another youth meeting was about to begin at *Beth Shalom*. Many young people were starting to arrive, and on this occasion our son, Oliver, came with his wife, Olga, and brought her cousin, Rafael, from Veracruz. This young man, 24, was still suffering from the trauma of seeing his father collapse and die on the spot from a heart attack, at 46 years of age, just three months prior. Oliver took me to the side, saying, "Pappy, I brought Rafael to you, because he needs a lot of prayer. He still suffers the pain and depression of losing his father."

So, Rafael and I went into a room alone to pray. As I prayed, laying hands on him, his body quivered and shook. And in a few minutes he was feeling much better. As we walked toward the door, before I laid my hand on the doorknob, the Spirit of God spoke to me, saying, *Stop. There is more. Have him lie down and pray over his heart.*

It was such a clear message that I could not mistake it. So I told him what the Lord had revealed to me. As he rested on the bed, I placed my hand over his heart and said, "In the name of Jesus, I am speaking to the spirit of heart congestion. You must come up and leave this heart right now!" It wasn't but about ten seconds, and a voice spoke through his mouth very clearly, "We are not going to leave his heart, because we have been assigned to him. Our master would destroy us!" they responded in the plural.

"What is your assignment?" I asked.

"To kill him! We are going to kill him! We killed his father, and now we have been assigned to kill him!" they spoke with a louder voice still.

"When did you come into him? You will tell me in Jesus' name."

"We came into him when we killed his father. With the trauma, we jumped into him," they boasted, "and we are going to kill him. We are going to kill him!" they continued to proclaim.

"No, you are going to come out right now, in the name of Jesus!" I said firmly.

"We hate you! We hate you!" they began to scream.

"I am so glad to hear that. Now you will leave this body and not delay any longer!" I informed them.

"Okay! We will go! But we will bring vengeance on you. You will see! Vengeance!"

"Get out, in the name of Jesus!" And with that last command, they began pulling loose. I had my hand still on Rafael's heart, and it began heaving and convulsing, causing him to choke and cough for several minutes. Then it all stopped, and Rafael came to consciousness.

"Wow!" he said. "I feel so good! Something terrible, something very heavy and painful came out of my chest. I feel so good now! What happened? I heard voices saying strange things about killing someone. What was it?"

I recounted the entire episode to him, and he began to remember all the words, but was unaware that these words were spoken by other entities through his mouth. He was well now, and as he stated, "Better than ever." And for the next four days, he shared his testimony with dozens of other young people at the meeting.

A Burning Retaliation

In March 2005, Lily and I were in the United States, ministering in California, and on our way back to Tulsa, we decided to go a few hours out of our way to visit with one of our sons and his family. That evening, a little before midnight, my cell phone rang. It was our other son, Philip, in Tulsa, and his voice sounded urgent.

"Pappy, your house is on fire!" he said. "There are several fire trucks here, and they can't contain the blaze. It is taking the whole house!"

In a very short time, we lost everything. The only possessions left were the clothes we had on and what was in the small suitcases we each had with us. At that moment, we both decided that we were not going to cry, but rather begin to praise the Lord because He was going to bring something important for His glory out of these seemingly horrible circumstances. At the same time, I thought about what the demon voices had said about taking vengeance, and as usual the enemy was trying to say to us, *See what you get for coming against my kingdom? But the Lord was saying to us, Trust Me. I have all things in My control.*

We thanked the Lord that He had showed us to go to our son's, instead of continuing straight through to our Tulsa home. We would have been sound asleep that night when the flames took over the century-old, two-story frame house, after apparently having started at a gas leak under the house. What made the circumstances even more difficult was the fact that, while we were busy in the work in Mexico, we had neglected to renew our fire insurance. Consequently, there were no funds with which to purchase another home. However, we still were very grateful that no one had been in the house, and that no surrounding homes were damaged.

After we arrived at what had been our home, I sat under a tree in the back, looking at the charred remains and prayed, "Lord, where do we go? We have no place now."

At that very moment, I saw our Christian neighbor walk over to greet me. He asked me to come with him to a furnished house he had a few doors away, and invited me inside.

"Would you like to stay here until you find a place?" he asked.

This was the Lord's instant answer to our prayers! May our Lord bless Bruce and Norma for this wonderful act of love and mercy. Indeed, the merciful shall obtain mercy (see Matt. 5:7).

Although we had almost no funds, we began looking for another house by faith. Then one day, suddenly, Philip and his wife, Roxana, found just the place. But the hard part would be to get a loan. Even with good credit, loan companies do not especially like to see "God" as your employer on the application. However, we kept praying, and believing, and finally it was approved, at a low interest rate. The Lord had once again showed His loving care to us, and many were the lessons of faith in the process.

MORE THREATS DEFEATED IN AN ANGELIC BATTLE

Soon, Lily and I found ourselves back at *Beth Shalom*, involved in another youth meeting and occupied with the many needs of the young people. One evening, she called me to come into the living room, and there together with the help of three of the cooks, she was delivering an 18-year-old girl from the spirits of witchcraft. Her parents had dedicated her to witchcraft when she was small. Now, the girl was writhing like a serpent on the floor and hissing. I sat on the sofa, and was just about to say something, when the girl sat up, and with glassy eyes, looked straight at me. I need to mention that this girl knew nothing about us, not even our names or from what country we came.

With those glassy eyes fixed on me, she reached out her hand and pointed to me, saying, "Listen, Levi! You listen! Wasn't it enough for you that we burned down your house in Tulsa, Oklahoma? Now you continue to pursue us! If you cast us out, we will burn down that house you just bought as well! Mark our word!" they threatened.

"If you get God's permission to do that, then He will give us a better house still," I replied. This made them very angry.

We have found through the years that spirits of witchcraft are powerful, and become deeply rooted in the person. On other occasions, we have learned that when this kind of stronghold continues to resist, we can call on God's angels to assist us, and soon we are seeing the battle come to a close, and victory at hand! This was the case here, and as soon as I began to pray aloud, "Heavenly Father, send us Your warrior angels to help us!" the demons shouted, "No! No! No! We don't want angels in here!" Nevertheless, they came within seconds. We could not see them, but there was suddenly what might be described as an electrically charged atmosphere. They apparently were carrying fiery swords, as they thrust them into her body. She grabbed her side, as though she were in deep pain, and the demons, using her hands, began to try to pull the sword out! Again and again this went on. We just sat there and watched, utterly amazed at what was transpiring. The cooks simply said, "This sure is different from being in the kitchen."

Then the girl stood up and began boxing the angels, saying, "Take that! Take that!" Suddenly, swords were again thrust into her sides, and the demons cried in pain. Continually, their number was reduced until they were all gone, and Caren was left lying on the floor, unconscious.

I put my fingers into a glass of water by my side, asked the Holy Spirit to use it, and sprinkled a few drops on her face. Immediately she sat up, and began to ask, "Where am I? Why am I on the floor?"

She remembered nothing, so my wife began to tell her all that had taken place. She knew nothing about Tulsa or a house fire. That evening, at midnight, Caren gave her heart to the Lord Jesus.

THE FATE OF SERPENTS

Our Lord tells us plainly, "I have sent you to tread upon serpents" (see Luke 10:19). These are spiritual serpents. Through the years, I have read to our children and then to our grandchildren, stories from a large children's Bible storybook. Inevitably, the picture of Adam and Eve in the Garden of Eden shows the serpent as a snake, hanging out of a fruit tree. In the beginning, the serpent was not a snake, but rather a beautiful, shining, wise, upright creature that the Lord had made. His name, in the original, means "the shining one." He was not satan himself, but loaned his body to satan and allowed him to speak through his mouth. There are a lot of people doing the same today. In essence, they have become antichrists. But the man of sin, the evil ruler to come, the antichrist of the Book of Revelation, will be satan himself, in human flesh. The first beast, the serpent, functions like the last beast, the antichrist, because they both have satan inside their flesh.

The serpent, or shining one, became the serpent we know today when God cursed him and said that from then onward, he would go on his belly and eat dust. Many people today have a fascination with serpents or snakes. The original serpent, or shining one, was made by the Lord God, but he was not made with the evil nature. The wicked nature came into him when he obeyed satan, when he became an accomplice in satan's plot to seduce Adam and Eve into disobeying God. Perhaps the serpent was offered an important position in satan's kingdom, should he gain it back.

Allow me to explain. Our Lord listed the serpents as one of the first beings that belonged to the kingdom of satan: "Behold, I give unto you power to tread on serpents and scorpions, and over all the power of the enemy" (Luke 10:19a). The only animal we find cursed by God at the time of the fall was the serpent, the snake as we know it, which has retained some of his design and beauty.

There is a prophecy in Isaiah 27:1 regarding the final doom of the serpent,

> *In that day the Lord with His sore and great and strong sword shall punish leviathan, the piercing serpent, even leviathan that crooked serpent; and He shall slay the dragon that is in the sea.*

The word *crooked* probably should be translated "writhing," referring to its ability to move in a waving manner, as a snake does to move about, or as belly dancers do to produce sexual seduction.

Satan has been allowed to take vengeance on us, but we are consoled by remembering three important things.

1. God is sovereign, which means that He is above all, and in control of all.

2. Vengeance against us is vengeance against the Lord. He will turn all things into His glorious purpose.

3. We are His children, the objects of His love, and as in the cases of Joseph and Job, He will always exonerate and reward us for our faithfulness.

ASK AND YOU SHALL RECEIVE

Realizing that our family pictures had been destroyed, the Lord consoled us—no one was hurt, only the pictures. Furthermore, my library of books had also been destroyed, including one very old, important Bible reference book, no longer in print! Now it too was gone. So, I prayed, "Lord, if there is any place on this earth where there is another copy of that book, please bring it into my hands."

Some months later while in the Yucatan, I was asked to speak to the leaders of a large church in the city of Merida. At the close of day, before I left, the pastor said to me, "Wait a moment, please," walked into his study, and came out with an old book in his hands. "This old book was in my grandfather's library," he said. "It is in English, and I don't know what it's about. I want you to have it." I looked at the book and realized it was a copy of the same book that I had lost in the fire!

How good of the Lord to look out after small details for us! He knew exactly where there was a copy, took me to a church I had never been to before, and caused the pastor to put his eyes on that one book, amongst hundreds of others, and bring it to my hands, just as I had asked Him. If you ask of Him an egg, He won't give you a scorpion (see Luke 11:10-13)!

Chapter Eighteen

GOD'S PRESENCE IN TRIALS

⚓

It is so wonderful to serve Jesus! His glorious presence is always with us when we walk with Him. Although, sometimes it is easy to forget about His presence when we are in the midst of trials, yet those times should be the sweetest times of all.

RUBBER, WATER, AND A GOOD MECHANIC

In 1982, we had just driven through Mexico City and were on our way to Guadalajara. About an hour out into the open desert, we began to smell water vapor coming into our '72 Chevrolet Suburban. I knew immediately that the odor was coming from our engine, so we pulled over to check under the hood. We discovered a water hose had broken, and unfortunately, I had nothing with which to replace it. There as a family, we sat in the middle of the desert, unable to move—just the Lord and us. So, we began to pray, "Lord, send us some help." In the meantime, I pulled out the dipstick to check the oil and discovered that the level of oil was above the "full" mark, and the color was like chocolate milk. I realized right away that the excess heat had cracked the head of the motor, and the water was mixing with the oil; hence, vapor was coming out the tailpipe.

Soon a car stopped behind us and a few people got out to see if they could help. Fortunately, they had some pieces of rubber with which to wrap the cracked water hose, and enough water to fill the radiator. We were grateful to our Lord, and thanked the kind people for being God's messengers. He had stopped the right vehicle.

Not long after we were back on the road, we began to notice the heat gauge slowly rising, and knew that in a few more miles the vehicle would be hot again. We began to pray aloud, "Lord, give us a container to carry water." While we prayed with our eyes on the road, a truck went speeding past us. Just then, from the opened back end, something red came flying out into the air—it was a large plastic container for carrying water! As the truck raced out of sight, the container flew to the side of the road, where we pulled right up next to it. Lily opened the door, and pulled it inside.

"Right on, Lord!" we said aloud, almost in unison, as we thanked Him.

About two miles ahead was a gas station, and there we filled both the radiator and the plastic container. By carrying extra water, we were able to reach Guadalajara without overheating again, and there we began to search for a good mechanic.

Within hours, God led a man to us who repaired the motor in good condition at a very moderate price, and at the same time, recommitted his life to the Lord, together with his family. Now we could see God's purpose in this trial.

"I am with you always," says our Lord, "even unto the end of the world" (Matt. 28:20b). Sometimes, though, it is easy to forget this wonderful promise, especially when we are in the midst of fiery trials.

GOAT'S MILK AND FIRECRACKERS

Many years ago while living in Chiapas, southern Mexico, our youngest child, Ruben, just six weeks old, could not digest his mother's milk any longer. We tried different formulas, but to no avail. So Lily began to try using the water from boiled pearl barley and rice to keep him alive. Yet he still continued to lose weight with each day that passed. As we went to the Lord to ask Him what to do, I began searching in that rural area amongst the neighboring ranches to see if there might be any goat milk. After a long search, I found just one goat, which a family was glad to lend to us. It gave very little milk, but Ruben enjoyed it, and actually, couldn't get enough of it. We were thankful to have it.

One evening about ten, as was my usual custom, I walked down the hill from the house to check on the goat where she was tied to a tree for lack of a pen. It was the rainy season, and she had lots of grass to eat. I arrived at the tree, turned my flashlight toward her, and saw that she was fine for the night. But before turning to go back up to the house, I noticed movement in the nearby bushes, and the form of a man's head. I quickly shut my light off, and immediately bullets began to fly. I made a dive for the tall grass, and crept along on my belly to a row of bushes that led me round about up to the house, where I dashed inside. Our baby, Ruben, was sleeping, but the rest of the family had heard the shots, and were beginning to feel panicky. I had caught sight of five men outside, not just one, all of whom carried guns. However, we had no physical weapons—only the Lord.

The phrase came to me, *The Lord is a very present help in the time of trouble* (see Ps. 46:1). "Thank You, Lord," I breathed; and then commanded in a hushed voice, "Everybody get down and lie on the floor." The wooden windows were shut, the door barred, and lights turned off. The shots toward the house continued, as we said, "Lord, protect us."

I was hoping that maybe a bolt of lightning would strike them dead, but it didn't. Instead, our daughter, Priscilla, found a bag of a thousand firecrackers and some matches.

"A man from the church brought these by, and said, 'Give these to your father, you might need them,'" she informed us. That we did! One by one I lit the firecrackers and slipped them under the door. They sounded just like gunshots. Meanwhile the shots from outside also continued, until finally around midnight the shots stopped. We had only a few firecrackers left when they decided to leave. Little Ruben had slept through the whole ordeal.

We sat up together on our chairs, and as a family, gave thanks to the Lord. He filled us again with His peace. "The thief comes to steal, kill, and destroy," (John 10:10) said our Lord. That had been the intention of these bandits. Satan meant to kill us, but once again, our Lord proved Himself faithful. The brother who brought the firecrackers later said to me, "I knew you didn't have any arms."

ATTACKED BY GUERILLAS

No one likes to be caught in dangerous places, yet sometimes things happen very suddenly. The enemy comes in like a flood; nevertheless, Jesus is always present when we walk with Him.

When we lived in Guatemala, the war took many lives and left many orphans. So-called "peace talks" were not producing peace, and it was not safe to travel at night. On one occasion, Lily stayed home, and I took three of my boys, a pastor, and his wife with me to minister in Guatemala City.

Then the day came to return home. It would be a six-hour trip, and we were getting a late start. Staying over in a hotel was out of the question because of the cost. So, at 6:00 P.M., we left the capitol; my son, Alfred, was driving. We stopped for some donuts on the way out, and prayed for the Lord's mercies as we went. Everyone was happy, rejoicing in a peaceful trip.

After traveling for a few hours, and coming to kilometer 126, my son Alfy stopped the vehicle and said, "Pappy, take the wheel. I'm getting sleepy." It was 10:00 P.M.

As I slipped into the driver's seat, it was a peaceful night. But with no moon, occasionally I put the lights on high beam to see farther ahead. "Thank You, Lord, for Your faithful protection," we told Him. At one point, I noticed kilometer 149 marked on a post. Then right after a blind curve, one of the boys remarked, "What are those lights ahead?" It looked like a campfire beside the road. Then my eyes caught sight of about 25 men with masks on their faces, and carrying machine guns. Guerillas!

As they ran toward us, I stepped on the brake and came to a stop about 100 feet from them. I quickly threw the gears in reverse, speeding backward as fast as possible. Those who were in the camper in back ducked down, so I could see out. Then, several of the guerillas opened fire on us as we tried to get away. As the shots continued, I could no longer see the line in the middle of the road behind me. Suddenly, my son Timothy shouted, "Stop! You are about to go over a cliff!" There was still an inch to go! And in that position we were able to turn around and flee, facing forward. We managed to get away, heading in the opposite direction, and thankful that no bullets had struck us.

Now, the question was how to stop the vehicles that we would be meeting along the way, so that they wouldn't fall into the same trap, and possibly be killed. The only way would be to position ourselves directly in front of them, while turning our high beams on and off. In this manner, we managed to stop cars, buses, and trucks, and inform them to turn around and seek shelter. Everyone understood and expressed their thanks.

When we reached a place where all the vehicles could be grouped together, I felt the Lord leading me to go aboard the buses and speak peace to them, praying for their salvation and safety in the name of Jesus. Everyone listened carefully, and each prayed.

It was midnight. Now, others were also helping to stop vehicles coming from Guatemala City. Then a big truck approached from the direction of the holdup, and the driver stopped to speak with me as I was standing beside the road. He informed me that several had been killed and that he had been held up for his money and his merchandise. Then, he said, "I saw the strangest thing! A blue pickup with a camper on back was approaching from Guatemala City. It came very close to the guerillas; then it started going backwards. I said to myself, I wish you luck! But you know, every time the guerillas fired at that truck, their machine guns went up into the air, as though pushed by some invisible force!"

"No wonder the bullets didn't hit us," I said. "That was our pickup! You see how God takes care of His own." I took time to witness to him, and to pray with him before he went on his way.

There was no sleep for most of us that night, but the Lord gave His Word of grace and comfort, as we spent the hours going from one vehicle to another, speaking to needy souls, and watching with prayer. It was a night of victory over the forces of darkness! Victory in Jesus!

Chapter Nineteen

WHAT IS ON THE HORIZON?

⚓

As my wife and I travel in the United States and in other countries, between conferences at *Beth Shalom*, we continually hear the questions: What is happening in our world? What will be next?

We are seeing the forces of good and the forces of evil advancing together. The day is far spent, and the night is upon us. Yet the darkness is causing even the smallest light to shine brighter, and the Spirit of God is stirring hearts of believers around the globe. A great spiritual awakening is on the rise, accompanied by wars, droughts, famines, pestilences, earthquakes, fear, greed, rebellion, and broken homes. These are the days that the Spirit of the Lord can work mightily through a few people who have fallen in love with Jesus; who have, like the grain of wheat, fallen into the ground and died (see John 12:24); and those who do not seek any part of the glory that belongs to Jesus.

THE FRUIT OF ONE LIFE

His eyes "run to and fro throughout the whole earth, to shew Himself strong in the behalf of them whose heart is perfect toward Him" (2 Chron. 16:9a). He is looking at every heart, and He is ready to do many mighty things on behalf of each one. He will accomplish through some, one hundredfold, through others sixty, and others thirtyfold (see Matt. 13:8). These are not percentages. One hundredfold is not one hundred percent. It means that one produces one hundred, which is 10,000 percent—a huge return on the investment of one life.

Our Lord made plain to us His plan for bearing fruit. He said, "He that abideth in Me, and I in him, the same bringeth forth much fruit: for without Me ye can do nothing" (John 15:5b). Bearing fruit does not come *from* us, but is accomplished *through* us. He said it aptly, "For without Me ye can do nothing." It is a natural outcome of abiding in His love. "Herein is My Father glorified, that ye bear much fruit; so shall ye be My disciples. As the Father hath loved Me, so have I loved you: continue ye in My love" (John 15:8-9).

Many years ago the Lord plainly said to me, *I will do for you all that you ask Me, if you abide in Me*. He has kept His promise, according to John 15:7, "If ye abide in Me, and My words abide in you, ye shall ask what ye will, and it shall be done unto you."

When we think of His Word abiding in us, we need to remember to meditate on it each day. He said, "The words that I speak unto you, they are spirit, and they are life" (John 6:63b). Stop here a moment and think on this: His Word is spirit! And it is life. We cannot have the filling of His Spirit if we are not filling ourselves with His Word.

DRINKING IN GOD'S WORD
AND DRAWING OUT THE WINE

You will recall the account of the first miracle that our Lord performed—the changing of water into wine at a wedding feast. It might have been a relative of His mother, Mary, who was getting married, because Mary was very concerned about the fact that the wine had run out, and knew that Jesus could do something about it. She was sure that this would be His opportunity to prove who He was. But it was not the Father's time yet.

Perhaps some people at the feast were aware that they were out of wine, but not all. And, moreover, not all desired it yet. To do the miracle at the hour that she wanted may have resulted in many people remaining unaware of the wine's origin. To produce it too soon would have avoided embarrassment for the host of the feast, but it probably would not have brought the same glory to God. Man's timing is often not God's timing. Sometimes embarrassment and discomfort are needed first, along with a proper thirst.

Jesus has told us, "I only do the things I see My Father do, and I only say the things I hear My Father say" (see John 5:19). This should also be our example. The right moment came, and Jesus pointed to six big water pots. Then He told the servants to go fill them to the brim. Six—man's number. That's us! He wants to use us. To be filled with what? Water. The water of God's Word, for His Word is spirit and is life. Yes, clay pots. That's us. The question is, are we available?

The servants filled them to the brim. There was no waving of His hands over them, no special speech. Just "Draw out now, and give to the host of the feast" (see John 2:8). Many are taking in God's Word, but they are not "drawing out." Yet it is in the drawing out that the water becomes wine! That is when the miracle takes place. When people taste of that wine, they will say, "This is the best I have ever tasted." This is the manner in which Jesus does His miracles through us. It is the simple obedience of abiding in His Word, and drawing out.

There is a little river that flows into the Sea of Galilee, and there is another little river that flows out from the sea—the

River Jordan. Galilee has always had fish in it. There is life. But the Jordan River, which flows into the Dead Sea, where there is no outlet, has no life in it. The Dead Sea is many times larger than the Sea of Galilee; likewise, the group of Christians who give nothing is much larger compared to the group who is always "drawing out." The Cessation Theology says, "These things have ceased." True! But the reason they have ceased in most places is because of unbelief. During Jesus' earthly ministry, miraculous works ceased in Nazareth because of unbelief. They claimed, "He's just the carpenter's son." But now today, in many places the Spirit of God is moving in hearts where new faith is being born. Don't be satisfied with taking in. Start giving it out. His Word is spirit and is life.

If God has blessed you materially, keep yourself from forming a love for possessions; keep them out of your heart. He has entrusted you with those blessings; as a good steward, ask Him where to channel them. His Spirit will flow through you if you do, giving you more abundantly, because of your faithfulness.

What is on the horizon today? God's Spirit is working mightily in many places. New wine is being experienced, and truly as in the Bible account, the latter wine will be superior to the former. It will become better than that of Pentecost, Wales, or Azusa Street. There will be nothing to equal it. It is on the way; however, it will be accompanied by hard times and persecution, by repentance and breaking of spirits, by continued wars and terrorism. His eyes are searching the whole earth today, looking for those whose hearts are perfect toward Him; He will not miss a single one.

When Elisha became the prophet who took up the mantle of Elijah, he received a double portion of Elijah's spirit; that is, a double measure. Even at the close of his life, when he died, there still remained the mighty power of the Holy Spirit in his bones, as we see from the story recorded in Second Kings 13:20-21.

Elisha had been buried for a year in a cave. One day nearby, several people were digging a grave to bury another man, when they looked up and saw a band of Moabite bandits coming. Before they fled, they grabbed the body and tossed it into the cave of Elisha's grave. When the body fell on the bones of Elisha, the man came to life and jumped to his feet! What a surprise for all of them!

Why would the Spirit of God still be in Elisha's bones after he had died? First, He had been in his bones while he was living. Second, because his body is going to be resurrected in the last day, as ours will be also. Hebrews 4:12 tells us that the Word of God is so powerful that it goes all the way into our bone marrow. These are not simply empty words. Recall the Lord's words, "My Word is spirit and is life" (see John 6:63).

Elisha fed his soul the Word of God, and that Word became spirit. Now we understand more why our Lord has told us to lay hands on the sick, and they shall recover. His Spirit is in the very bones of the one who is abiding in Him, and feeding on His Word. His Word is also life, and brings life to others. You need not expect many healings in others if you do not follow His orders. The miracles take place only when there is obedience: Go. Preach. Heal. Cast out demons. Once the Word has entered you, you must "draw out," and the rivers of the Holy Spirit will begin to flow.

A Choice of Commitment and Death

The child of God who wants God to use him cannot fill his life with the things that feed his flesh nature. Therefore, we must allow the Holy Spirit to search our hearts. He will reveal the things that are harmful to our spiritual life. Sometimes it is not easy to rid ourselves of these things, simply because they are the very things that bring pleasure to the flesh. This is the reason that our Lord said, "If any man will come after Me, let him deny himself, and take up his cross daily, and follow Me" (Luke 9:23b).

It is this matter of denying ourselves that makes many would-be followers stop in their tracks. Some say to themselves, "I think I will put dying to self on hold." Others decide that a life of self-denial is just not for them. Still others are "stop and start," until they decide which they love more—Jesus or themselves. Decisions must be made, and even as you read this, you are deciding, or have decided, whether you will live in death to self and total self-denial, or not. He will not allow you to manipulate His will. Either you surrender all, or none at all. May the blessed Holy Spirit of God help you in this moment to make that full commitment.

There is a peace that passes all understanding awaiting you, and blessings without end for every day of your life. Allow Him to be in control, the loving Savior, who gave His life for you. Don't let the enemy cause you to postpone such an important decision, as he will then harden your heart, and offer you what he cannot give. He continues to operate as "the god of this world" until his time expires (see 2 Cor. 4:4). And until then, he is allowed to "sift" us "as wheat," as the Lord said to Peter (see Luke 22:31). This sifting process is for sorting out believers in order to define which course their lives will take—of total obedience with abundant blessings, of partial obedience with partial blessings, or of disobedience with no blessings. The choice is yours, and that choice will be tested.

Chapter Twenty

THE POWER OF PRAYER, PEACE, AND TWO BY TWO

⚓

Through the years, we have learned several things about taking the Gospel to families and homes. Indeed, I would have been blessed if someone had shared these things with me from the beginning. Thus, I now pass them along to you.

TWO BY TWO WITH PRAYER

First, the Lord sent the disciples out two by two, and He had a good reason to do so. Assumedly, spiritual power is doubled with two people. However, this is not the case. Actually, it is ten times as great, for there is a spiritual law that says, "One shall put a thousand to flight, and two shall put ten thousand to flight" (see Deut. 32:30). Our Lord clearly said, "...if two of you shall agree on earth as touching any thing that they shall ask, it shall be done for them of My Father which is in heaven" (Matt. 18:19). This is literally a guarantee to us.

So two can go out with ten times the power over the enemy, and as they do, they are assured of receiving anything that they ask of the Father. What a glorious way to live! Agree on salvation for a household; agree on healing for the sick; agree on deliverance for the oppressed; agree on God's provision for you and others. And watch it happen before your very eyes, giving praise to the One who paid for it all with His own precious blood. Let the words of Paul always be present: "He that spared not His own Son, but delivered Him up for us all, how shall He not with Him also freely give us all things?" (Rom. 8:32).

Second, before going out together to preach His Word, meet together for prayer, to be filled with His Spirit, to ask for His direction and wisdom, and to bind the power of the enemy before you reach the homes.

PEACE

Third, when arriving at a home, pronounce peace upon it before entering. Jesus gave good instructions, yet they are seldom observed. "And into whatsoever house ye enter, first say, Peace be to this house. And if the son of peace be there, your peace shall rest upon it: if not, it shall turn to you again" (Luke 10:5-6). Notice that this Scripture is a command—that we should bless a home with *our* peace. He has said, "My peace I give unto you" (John 14:27b). This peace is not just an empty word. When you have *His peace*, you know it. And if you don't have it, you should realize you need it. Then it is yours, and you can give it, as He gave it to you.

Peace is one of the fruits of the Holy Spirit, and a part of the very nature of God. He is the God of all peace, yet there are not many homes where there is peace. So, if there is no peace, how are they able to hear the Word of the Lord? You hold the key to that home. When you speak peace to that home, immediately God's Spirit surrounds it with peace; and all the anxieties, distractions, fears, and doubts are extracted from those walls, because by *your* authority, God's peace has moved in. If the Son of peace sees them worthy, then you are to leave your peace with them. If they are not worthy, then you are to remove your peace from that house. We carry with us the most precious treasure that the world is looking for. While the devil offers a false sense of peace, Jesus offers the real thing. How blessed we are to be His custodians of it, and have the authority to bestow it, and to remove it.

Speaking peace to a home makes a grand difference. Hearts become immediately peaceful, and those living there begin to listen with great interest. Even a household of people deemed unworthy become better listeners. However, if they continue to reject our Savior, we cannot leave such a blessing for them to enjoy. It needs to be removed.

Our Lord, by the use of His commands to us, has helped us to understand that peace is not just a word. It is an immeasurable spiritual blessing that can be extended over everything that the family does—if they are worthy. This blessing is ours to enjoy and to give to others.

Jesus spoke peace to His disciples two times upon meeting them after His resurrection, in the room where they had locked themselves for fear of the Jews. It was not just a word or a greeting, but an actual transference of His peaceful nature. The first time seems to have dealt with removing the shock of seeing Him walk through that closed door. The second time was to prepare them for a very important announcement. "Then said Jesus to them again, Peace be unto you: as My Father hath sent Me, even so send I you" (John 20:21).

THE AUTHORITY GIVEN TO EVERY BELIEVER

To help them understand the impact of His statement, He breathed on them, and said, "Receive ye the Holy Ghost" (John 20:22b). The full meaning of His announcement is still not grasped by many today: "As My Father hath sent Me, even so send I you." It does not simply mean, "He sent Me, and I send you." The real meaning is in doing the things that Jesus did. And what did Jesus do? He preached; He healed; and He cast out demons.

In the Book of Acts, we find the apostles doing the same three things. They understood His command, with the help of the Holy Spirit from His breath, and again, by the coming of the Holy Spirit upon them at Pentecost. He knew that this command was so important that they would need an extra unction from His breath to grasp it.

Wherever the Gospel is being preached, together with the healing of the sick and casting out of evil spirits, there is a very rapid increase in the harvest of souls for Jesus in that area. Sometimes it is an area that has previously heard the Gospel repeatedly, but has never experienced the confirmation of His power and authority that is seen in the compassion that He has for those who are sick and oppressed by satan. When we read His Word, we are amazed at what Jesus did; yet somehow, we are unable to comprehend these things happening today. Or, if we do see evidence of them happening, we remain doubtful as to whether or not we ourselves can heal others and cast out demons.

So often today, we hear a commercialized expression, "What would Jesus do?" But it is necessary to first ask ourselves, "What *did* Jesus do?" And this should then become the pattern of what we do.

Frequently someone will say to me, "But I don't have the gift of healing or the gift of casting out demons." First of all, let it be understood that the casting out of demons is not on the list of gifts. It is not a gift. It is the authority given to every believer, found in the Great Commission (see Mark 16:17-18). You are to rely on the power of the name of Jesus. Secondly, there are gifts of healing for believers to be used in the Body of Christ (see 1 Cor. 12:9). However, the practice of healing is also found in the Great Commission, which is for all believers. We cannot escape these obvious commands.

The Holy Spirit is moving today to shake us loose from our complacency, to open our eyes to see the fields which are white unto harvest, and to empower us to speak His Word, heal the sick, and cast out evil spirits. If we are afraid of failure, let us ask our Lord's forgiveness, and remember that "...perfect love casteth out fear" (1 John 4:18a).

Chapter Twenty-one

WORDS OF CAUTION

⚓

Beloved reader, as you read these lines, the prayer of my heart is that your eyes will be turned to Jesus. Our heavenly Father does not want us to focus on men and women, who are simply the channels through which He works.

When Jesus was transfigured on the mountain before three of His disciples and His clothing radiated His glory, the whole scene filled them with amazement. That is, until Moses and Elijah appeared, and the attention shifted to them! Indeed, they were awestruck by seeing the two Old Testament prophets. Peter, the usual spokesman, wanted these special men to stay around for a while, perhaps as guest conference speakers. He placed the same importance on them, equating them with Jesus, and suggested making three tabernacles to house them. But our Father above was displeased with their change of focus, and He sent a cloud over them through which He spoke, "This is *My beloved Son*, in whom I am well pleased; *hear ye Him*" (Matt. 17:5b, emphasis added; see also verses 1-8). The Father could not keep silent, because man, instead of God, was about to receive the glory.

I beg of you, see only Jesus. Hear Him and obey Him.

DEPEND ONLY ON GOD

In 1994, when I was on the southern island off Cuba, in a home meeting, I met a young man who stuttered so much that I needed great patience to comprehend what he was saying. Finally, his request made sense—He wanted to preach God's Word, but he could not be understood. As I prayed in my heart to know what to do, the Spirit of God led me to anoint the tip of his tongue with oil, and then for him to shout "Hallelujah!" as loudly as he could. The word came out loud and clear. And from that very moment the stuttering was gone! To this day, Mario is preaching the Word of God throughout that island, and the rest of Cuba as well. He is also doing the works that Jesus did. When he finds someone who stutters, he anoints his or her tongue, and tells them to shout "Hallelujah!" Consequently, they are released as he was. We rejoice that he was set free.

One of the lessons that God has impressed on us is to insist that people not form a dependency on us, but to go directly to Him. And when others are healed or delivered by their ministry in turn, they should likewise teach people to do the works of Jesus, and not depend on them. God's work is to be multiplied and Jesus is to be glorified. The three things that Jesus did are the charge that is given to *every* believer, not just a chosen few. We keep His words before us: "As My Father hath sent Me, even so send I you" (John 20:21b).

On that same southern island there was brought to me a woman who had suffered 14 years with daily migraine headaches, which frequently made her think of taking her life. Susana had forgotten what it felt like to not have a headache.

This dear lady had previously been told that the migraines were probably caused by badly infected teeth, so several of them had been removed to see if that would help. It didn't. Other doctors performed experiments on her, but nothing helped. She lived in the farthest town on the eastern tip of Cuba proper, and when hearing of our arrival on the adjacent island, she traveled by whatever means available for three days to reach Havana, and from there took a boat to the smaller island, arriving the day before we were to leave.

When I met Susana, she had both hands on her head, and her facial expression was one of extreme pain. As soon as my son Abram and I laid hands on her, there was an immediate reaction from within her, even before I could utter a word. The angry voice said, "We're not coming out! She belongs to us!"

"What is your name?" I inquired.

"Migraine!" came the answer.

Abram and I insisted that it leave in Jesus' name, and it left in a convulsive cough that lasted about three minutes. Then she was free, totally free!

Susana has since written us two letters during the last several years, telling us that she has never suffered another migraine. Now, God is using her to take healing to others. These things warm our hearts, because we see, time after time, that common people, not religious people, but those with the faith of a child, take hold of His commands, and they, too, are seeing Him fulfill His promises.

I want to clarify here that we don't mean to imply that all migraine headaches are caused by migraine spirits; however, we have found in our ministry that there are a considerable number of them. Others seem to have a physiological cause, which God will also heal.

Our hearts are filled with joy when we see people healed of in-firmities, and others set free from satan's power. We know and live what our Lord has said:

> *Behold, I give unto you power to tread on serpents and scor-pions, and over all the power of the enemy: and nothing shall by any means hurt you. Notwithstanding in this rejoice not, that the spirits are subject unto you; but rather rejoice, be-cause your names are written in heaven* (Luke 10:19-20).

REJOICE FOR THE RIGHT REASON

Here is another word of caution to us from our Lord: to rejoice that the spirits are subject unto us leads to pride and self-glory. It is far better to rejoice in having our names written in Heaven. This is something for us to always be thinking about.

We should rejoice when we witness someone being set free from the captivity of the enemy. It is likened, perhaps, to one who goes into the enemy's territory, kills several of the enemy's war-riors, and finds his brother, unties him from a post, and escapes with him to freedom. He rejoices because his brother is free. He is no longer held captive. This is proper rejoicing.

Improper rejoicing would be to return with your brother, re-joicing that you were the one who had rescued him and you were the one who had put the enemy under foot to do so.

The same is true of healing. Healing comes from Jesus, and Him alone. "With His stripes we are healed" (Isa. 53:5b). "Bless the Lord, O my soul, and forget not all His benefits: who forgiveth all thine iniquities; who healeth all thy diseases; who redeemeth thy life from destruction; who crowneth thee with lovingkindness and tender mercies; who satisfieth thy mouth with good things; so that thy youth is renewed like the eagle's" (Ps. 103:2-5). It is Jesus who heals. Only Jesus!

SATAN USES RELIGION

When we begin to do the works of Jesus, there will most certainly be opposition from the enemy, and it often comes from sources that we least expect. So, here is another word of caution: The Lord will use you mightily, and you can certainly rejoice with those who have been healed and delivered from satan's power. However, be ready for satan's slander. Jesus was both slandered and persecuted for the miracles that He did on earth. Who did these things against Him? The religious rulers and religious people of His day. They hated Him, and every time they heard of another miracle or of someone declaring that He was the Son of God, they hated Him more, to the point of wanting to kill Him. Hence, Jesus would frequently command the demons to be quiet, so that the rulers would not be provoked even more to get rid of Him before His appointed time.

Sometimes we ask a demon a question, as Jesus did, but only in order to use the information against him. People say that demons always lie. No, they don't always. For example, one said to Jesus, "I know Thee who Thou art, the Holy One of God" (Mark 1:24b). Interestingly, demons knew who Jesus was, but the theologians did not. "And He healed many that were sick of divers diseases, and cast out many devils; and suffered not the devils to speak, because they knew Him" (Mark 1:34).

Today, we have a similar problem. When God is working by His Spirit, healing the sick, and setting captives free, you can be sure that someone within the religious ranks will come against it. Denominational pride is alive and well. Many times in home meetings we have experienced a glorious presence of the Lord in our midst as we worship Him, which produces an atmosphere for some marvelous healings. But sooner or later, announcements are made in some churches telling members to beware of these meetings, because "they are not approved by our denomination." Defamations flow, even though no investigations are ever made on their part. Here is where we need to let the Lord handle the matter, and pray for those who condemn us. The Word says, "He that loveth not knoweth not God; for God is love" (1 John 4:8). It is difficult to love those who speak evil of us, but it is required of us; and if we are not able to do this, we may soon lose the authority that He has given to us.

The apostle Paul had a problem with carnal Christians in one church, but he was still able to love them. Speaking of satan's tactics, he said, "We are not ignorant of his devices" (2 Cor. 2:11b); unlike today, there does seem to be considerable ignorance in these matters. There came a time when all had forsaken him, except Luke. Luke was a doctor, but is never found practicing medicine in the Scriptures, but rather helping Paul in keeping records of the works of the Holy Spirit through the apostles.

Once you have been criticized or defamed by those who should love you, turn your eyes again upon Jesus, and keep them there, or you will go down. He will never leave you or forsake you. In our work in Latin America, there are some pastors and Christian workers, who once severely criticized us, but are now doing the works of Jesus; consequently, their ministries have begun to grow rapidly. In turn, many of them are now receiving criticism, and we find ourselves encouraging them.

It is when we do the works that Jesus did that the Gospel prospers. Every believer in the congregation needs to understand how he can do these things. They need to be taught even as a son is taught by his father, or a daughter by her mother. They will see it and do it with you as a pastor, until it becomes second nature to them. It will become a hands-on experience for each one who participates, and the blessings will begin to come upon them as the Spirit of God flows through them. We are forever grateful to our Lord for the many things He has taught us in this process of learning to obey Him. It is a life of His abiding presence, for He has said, "...and, lo, I am with you always, even unto the end of the world" (Matt. 28:20), a promise that is given to those who go and do His works.

Chapter Twenty-two

WHAT ABOUT THE GIFTS
OF THE SPIRIT?

⚓

Preach, heal, and cast out demons—these three responsibili-
ties represent the authority given to every believer by our Lord
Himself, and are authorized by the name which is above all
names—the name of Jesus (see Phil. 2:9). When we use His
name, it is as though Jesus Himself is speaking. This is the authority that His name carries.

The apostle Paul gives us much of the teaching that we use in
the Church today. But what the Holy Spirit has given us through
Paul does not mean that we should throw out what has been given
in the Gospels or the Old Testament; rather, this teaching is
meant to clarify and build upon it.

In First Corinthians 12, we find the main teaching regarding
the gifts given to us by the Holy Spirit through the apostle Paul.
We need to understand the reason for the gifts and the use of
each one. Paul says that there is one body with many members
(see 1 Cor. 12:12). If the members of our physical body are

coordinated together, the purpose of life is carried out. So it is spiritually. There are nine spiritual gifts to be used in the spiritual body, placed into three categories—*three,* the number of resurrection power.

I. Gifts of Speaking.

    a. Tongues.

    b. Interpretation of Tongues.

    c. Prophecy.

II. Gifts of Knowledge

    a. Word of Knowledge.

    b. Word of Wisdom.

    c. Discerning of Spirits.

III. Gifts of Power.

    a. Diving Healing.

    b. Miracles.

    c. Faith.

Notice that there are three groups of three, for a total of nine. We realize also that there are nine fruits of the spirit. Each fruit flows from the first one—love.

1. Love—the very essence of God, for "God is love" (1 John 4:8b).

2. Joy—God's love overflowing within us.

3. Peace—God's love removing all fear and anxiety.

4. Longsuffering—God's love giving us the ability to carry out His plans until they are accomplished.

5. Gentleness—God's love in human character.

6. Goodness—God's love in human deeds.

7. Faith—God's love empowering us to act on His promises and commands.

8. Meekness—God's love removing man's pride.

9. Temperance—God's love keeping all thoughts, words, and deeds in balance with His nature.

It is not enough to know the use of each gift of the Spirit or to understand where our place is within that structure. Indeed, the gifts can only operate properly when they are thoroughly controlled by the fruit of the Spirit. In addition, the fruit of the Spirit will not be in production until the "seed," which is our life, is planted in the ground and dies. Then it can bear "much fruit" (see John 12:24-25).

Notice that the whole structure of fruit-bearing is built on the love of God. "The fruit of the Spirit is love" (Gal. 5:22). And God is love. Out of love flows the other eight fruits. Three is the square root of nine; and three is the number of resurrection (three days in the tomb), the number of the Trinity in Heaven (that is, the third Heaven). It is, thus, the number of power. The power of the resurrection times the power of the Trinity equals nine, the fruit of the Spirit, which is to function in the Body, through the nine gifts of the Spirit.

THE SPEAKING GIFTS: TONGUES

The writer, James, says that a person's tongue is like the helm (rudder) of a great ship, which even though it is so small, can turn a huge vessel around. Such is the tongue, turning the course of one's life to go in the opposite direction. James also says that the tongue can be lit with the fire of hell (see James 3:6).

In the Book of Acts, chapter 2, the Holy Spirit came at Pentecost and brought tongues of fire, which caused them to begin speaking in other tongues. It was the fire of the Holy Spirit, as was promised in Luke 3:16. The tongue can be set on fire from above.

It is the heavenly fire of God's holiness, the same fire that struck a bush before Moses' eyes without consuming it. The unusual fire that burned so beautifully without harming the bush fascinated Moses to the point that he moved closer to see how this could be. But God stopped him and commanded him to remove his shoes, for he was standing on holy ground. His shoes had been acting as insulators, whereas his bare feet needed to have direct contact with that holy ground. When he did so, the awareness of God's holiness came upon him, and caused him to hide his face, out of holy reverence for God (see Exod. 3:1-6).

This is what is missing in our lives today—a touch of His purifying holiness. We are fascinated with the fire, but as we come closer to it and walk on holy ground, we still wear the insulators on our feet. Consequently, His holiness does not reach our feet, much less our tongues. We need, at this point, to pray the prayer of David: "Search me, O God, and know my heart: try me, and know my thoughts: and see if there be any wicked way in me, and lead me in the way everlasting" (Ps. 139:23-24).

Often, we are like Moses, who kept moving closer to God's fire. It seemed the proper thing to do, but it had not occurred to him that he needed to remove his shoes. If we have hindrances in our lives, God's fire cannot purify us.

Perhaps you are insulating yourself from the touch of God's holy fire. Find out what it is, because no matter how close you draw to that fire, you will not be touched by it until you deal with that matter that has come between you and God.

Isaiah did not know that he had unclean lips until he had a vision of the Lord in His glory, high and lifted up (see Isa. 6:1-8). He, like most of us, was ignorant of his inner condition; but upon seeing the glory of God, he cried out, "Woe is me! for I am undone; because I am a man of unclean lips, and I dwell in the midst of a people of unclean lips: for mine eyes have seen the King, the Lord of hosts" (Isa. 6:5).

Our language can be considered appropriate by all those around us, yet be unclean—that is, not touched by God's holiness. Isaiah was so shocked by what he perceived of his condition that he cried out, "Woe is me, for I am undone! Because I am a man of unclean lips."

When God sees that we recognize our condition, He responds immediately to our need, as He did to Isaiah when He sent one of the seraphim from the altar with a live coal to put on his lips, and remove the sin and guilt.

Those who were waiting in the upper room for Pentecost had seen the Lord of glory die before their eyes. Their hearts were broken, and now they had been fasting and praying for ten days, which prepared them for receiving the Holy Spirit upon them. Then the holy fire of God touched their tongues, and they were filled with the Holy Spirit. We, too, desperately need to see our bankrupt condition so that the Lord will touch us and our tongues with His holiness and power. Anything less than this will be false holiness of our own making, which is an abomination to the Lord.

In First Corinthians 14, the apostle Paul explains the threefold purpose of tongues. They are:

1. To edify oneself (see 1 Cor. 14:4).
2. To edify the Church, with the use of an interpreter (see 1 Cor. 14:5).
3. To be a sign to unbelievers (see 1 Cor. 14:22).

There are some needs within our spirits that haven't been met and often those needs are so deep that the power of God has to go directly into our spirits by the use of another tongue from the Holy Spirit. Our spirits receive the touch, even though our understanding is left untouched. Here is where Paul says we can ask the Lord for the meaning, and He will give that also (see 1 Cor. 14:13-15).

Our tongues can become powerful instruments when the Holy Spirit flows through them, but our spirits must be touched first. When we line up with Him, He will cleanse us thoroughly on a daily basis. He wants His rivers of living water to flow through us, with our tongues being the source of those rivers; and which if we don't surrender to the Lord, will become like the serpent's tongue, divided in two, and ready to speak from the flesh and the devil at the same time. Many churches have an atmosphere that hinders the Holy Spirit, simply because of a few individuals who allow these two enemies to bring satan's poison into their midst.

INTERPRETATION OF TONGUES AND PROPHECY

When the gift of interpreting tongues is used in the church, or within any group of believers, that which the Holy Spirit gives in another tongue actually becomes prophecy. Without an interpreter, it is not to be spoken before the group, but should be kept as a personal prayer with the Lord (see 1 Cor. 14:27-28).

Paul places the gift of prophecy on an important level. Many Christians think that prophecy is mostly prediction, but that is its lesser purpose. In First Corinthians 14:3, the apostle Paul defines *prophecy* as "edification, exhortation, and consolation." He does not mention prediction, though it was used by prophets, especially in the Old Testament.

Paul provides us with wise counsel in First Thessalonians 5:20-21. "Despise not prophesyings. Prove all things; hold fast that which is good." Many believers have decided to discontinue the use of the gift of prophecy because of misuse. Frequently, predictions have been given that never came to pass, which has caused people to turn away from the gift. However, we are encouraged to retain that which is good. So we need to pray for wisdom and discernment when we hear prophecy, whether it is for edification, exhortation, or consolation; and in the nature of prediction, even more care is required. Those who give false predictions are not prophets and are not considered God's mouthpiece.

WORD OF KNOWLEDGE

The gift of knowledge is used on occasion. It is an immediate revelation that is given to solve a problem or give direction. God's Spirit gave Elisha a word of knowledge about his servant Gehazi when that servant followed after Naaman. Elisha was shown where Gehazi had gone and why. Gehazi's heart was filled with avarice, which needed to be dealt with (see 2 Kings 5).

Oftentimes when my wife and I are ministering deliverance to someone, the Holy Spirit brings a word of knowledge to one of us, or sometimes to both, which is a major key to helping that person become free from satan's power. Sometimes it is the revelation of a disease that the person didn't know he had. Having that word of knowledge from the Lord is evidence that it will be removed upon command, in the name of Jesus.

A few years ago in Mexico, I was asked to pray for a young man who had a brain tumor that was paralyzing him, and left him unable to work and support his wife and two children. He could barely get around by holding on to the wall, and he was told that an operation would not be successful. As I prayed over Mateo, I did not receive any special revelation from the Lord. He did feel somewhat better, but most of the symptoms were still there. For the rest of the day, as I visited other families, his need was ever before me in prayer.

The following morning, I awoke suddenly before dawn. It seemed that the Lord wanted to tell me something. As I began to inquire of Him, He gave me a partial word of knowledge about Mateo, saying, *Go back to Mateo, and ask him if he is left-handed.* I was truly surprised by this word, and said, "Lord, what will I do with that information?" and He answered, *Just go and ask him that, and I will lead you in what is to follow.* The directions were clear, but I couldn't yet make any sense of them, and, to tell the truth, I wondered how it was all going to turn out.

Once again at Mateo's house, I found him glad to see me. "Mateo," I said, "I have returned to ask you a question." He looked at me, wondering what it might be. "The Lord has told me to ask you if you are left-handed," I said without hesitation.

"Wow! That is sure an interesting question," he replied. "Yes, I am." The Lord then led me a step at a time in this strange word of knowledge.

"Mateo, did you ever hit your wife with that left hand?" I continued.

"No, but I felt like it, because I found her looking at other men. Instead, I smashed my fist into that plate glass window!" He pointed to the huge window that had since been replaced.

Before I could ask Mateo about what reactions he felt in his hand or arm upon hitting the glass, he commented, "You know, now it comes back to me! When I struck that glass, I was angry, and I felt that anger go up my arm like a current, and into my head. My head has felt different ever since."

The Lord continued with the word of knowledge. "That spirit of anger, Mateo, has formed a nest for itself in your brain, and that nest has become a massive tumor," I said.

Mateo began to ask God's forgiveness. I knew that time could not be wasted, and with one hand on his head, and the other on his left arm, I ordered it out.

"In Jesus' name, the spirit of anger that came in through Mateo's fist, went up his arm, and into his head, will be uprooted and come out of him right now. In Jesus' name. No part of you will remain in his head or in any part of his body!"

Immediately, Mateo's head and body began to shake violently, and finally just the left hand was shaking, until that also stopped. Mateo knew that he was healed. The partial paralysis was gone, and he could walk normally. All of his sense of feeling had returned, and the heavy dense feeling in his head was gone.

I then invited Mateo to the evening service in the church, and he promised to come. During the daytime, the word had gotten around about his healing, and an extra large crowd turned out. The music of praise had begun when Mateo walked in. He began to dance before the Lord in praise and gratitude, which brought in a spirit of revival for the glory of God. Let me add that Mateo continues in good health, and God's peace abides on their family. The whole church experienced the spiritual renewal from this marvelous testimony.

WORD OF WISDOM

The gift of wisdom is different from the gift of knowledge, for wisdom is skill in the use of knowledge. King Solomon asked God for wisdom to rule His people, and it was given to him. James says, "If any of you lack wisdom, let him ask of God, that giveth to all men liberally, and upbraideth not; and it shall be given him" (James 1:5). This is a marvelous resource that God has set forth before each of us, His children. However, this Scripture is not referring to the gift of wisdom, or word of wisdom, as it is called.

The word of wisdom is given to a few within the Body of Christ. It is given only to those with a humble and contrite spirit, to those who have learned to fear the Lord. "The fear of the Lord is the beginning of wisdom: and the knowledge of the Holy is understanding" (Prov. 9:10). One who has the gift of wisdom is aware of possessing it, but does not declare it. He knows that it functions only as he humbles himself continually before the Lord, for both wisdom and meekness are the character of Christ. If the gift of wisdom were entrusted to a person who tends toward pride, the glory would probably not go to the One who bestowed it, the Lord Jesus.

This special gift of wisdom, placed in the Body of Christ, is for special needs, where there doesn't seem to be a solution on the horizon for a particular problem or need. With the gift of wisdom, one has the ability to see into and understand the situation at hand, and subsequently enables others to understand it as well. That person does not rely on prudence, common knowledge, or book learning, nor does he seek man's approval—only God's.

Certainly, Solomon demonstrated the use of the gift of divine wisdom from the very start in the case of the two women who claimed the same baby (see 1 Kings 3:16-28).

DISCERNING OF SPIRITS

The gift of discerning of spirits is far more necessary in the Body of Christ than is thought. It is not a gift of casting out spirits, though that can accompany it. There is no such gift as the "casting out of spirits" on the list of gifts. That is the authority of every believer, as shown in the Great Commission (see Mark 16:15-18). The gift of discerning of spirits is just what it says. The Holy Spirit enables those with this gift to discern the presence of evil spirits in people and in teachings. Paul shows us an example when he lists some "doctrines of demons" (see 1 Tim. 4:1-5). Also, we find that he discerned a demon spirit of divination in a girl, which he then did cast out (see Acts 16:16-24). This cost him and Silas many stripes, and they were thrown in jail for setting her free.

Every church needs a person or two, at least, with this gift, for most Christians are unable to discern the presence of spirits, to distinguish their functions and their names. When these facts are known, it becomes much easier to remove them, as the declaration of their names to them begins to break their stronghold. Many churches have been destroyed for the lack of the knowledge and function of the gifts, especially this one, the discerning of spirits. Satan has spirits assigned especially to those churches that remain ignorant of this important gift. If that ignorance remains, they will eventually destroy that church.

DIVINE HEALING

This brings us to the third group: the gifts of power—gifts of healing, the gift of miracles, and the gift of faith. The first, gifts of healing, is plural, seeming to indicate that there are variations within the gift itself. We have noticed through ministering in different places of the world, that some believers with this gift seem to have a specialized area of healing, and others work in all areas of healing. But let us not forget, as we have noted before, that the authority to heal is also found in the Great Commission for every believer.

At this point, once again, let me encourage you to stretch forth your hands, lay them on the sick, and in the holy name of Jesus, command the infirmity by its name (migraine, diabetes, asthma, etc.) to leave the body and not return. Take authority over it, and command it out, in Jesus' name! You are in for some wonderful surprises.

But, then, why are these "gifts of healing" registered on this list, as well? Our Lord is even more concerned about the body. He does not want us to be without the means of healing, and has even given a great variety of gifts within this one administration. See what Paul says by the Holy Spirit in First Corinthians 12:4-7.

Now there are diversities of gifts, but the same Spirit. And there are differences of administrations, but the same Lord. And there are diversities of operations, but it is the same God which worketh all in all. But the manifestation of the Spirit is given to every man to profit withal.

Just as there are different kinds of apples and different kinds of grapes in the natural world, so it is in the spiritual realm. There are various modes of operation within the administration of healing.

Within our own ministry, my wife and I have a similar, yet different modes of operation. It is so good, I believe, that He didn't make us exactly alike.

In a city on the Gulf Coast of Mexico, we were visiting a Christian family in their home. One of the sisters, named Dalia, had been a nurse, but now, unable to walk, was confined to a wheelchair. This time, the Spirit of God impressed upon me to do things differently. We simply laid hands on her, thanked the Lord for her healing, and told her that at eight the next morning we would wait for her at the church three blocks away, where she would walk to on her own. That is exactly what happened, and we rejoiced together there at the church, giving thanks to our Lord for her healing. Since that day in 1993, Dalia has been in good health, serving the Lord, and laying healing hands on others.

MIRACLES

This gift is not seen very often in the Western Hemisphere at the present time, but it is there; whereas, miracles take place with more frequency in lesser developed countries. Many who do not travel are unaware of what God is doing to reveal Himself to those who are to come into His family. What a boost it has been to our faith to see His hand at work through His babes in the faith. If we remain open in our hearts, and do not limit within our minds what we think God will or will not do, He will turn spiritual children into our teachers. We do need to learn from them, and that learning will be deep and lasting.

One of the biographies that impressed me the most as I was growing up, was that of Samuel Morris, a young lad who was born in Liberia, West Africa, whom God brought to America over a century ago. Samuel was of such simple, pure faith, that his life made a strong impact wherever he went. The fruit of that life continues to be in evidence today.

We, as a family, have seen the hand of the Lord working miracles on our behalf. It would take another book to list them all. But why is the term "gift of miracles" used? In Acts 19:11-12, we find Paul doing certain miracles, as there were no doubt more people who needed healing than he could attend, so he sent them handkerchiefs and aprons that he had prayed over. It produced, in many people, both healing and deliverance from evil spirits. This is happening today. Miracles are needed more now than ever before, and there are those whom God has chosen today to be instruments of His miracles. Keep your heart open to the Holy Spirit, and don't let the "commercialization" of these things cause you to lose God's blessings. Satan is a clever thief.

During Jesus' life, the people of Nazareth didn't see many of His miracles, because of their large-scale unbelief. Likewise, there seem to be many "Nazareths" today. But when there is a town that chooses to believe, God's Spirit can do mighty things there.

In southern Mexico, near Guatemala, there is a town of over four thousand souls who formerly lived in spiritual and moral darkness. When God's servants entered there with the Gospel and with much prayer, they won the people's hearts to Jesus, not simply by the preaching of the Gospel, but because the signs and wonders of healing, deliverance, and miracles accompanied the Word. Today, most of the town professes faith in Christ, and visitors can hear the townspeople addressing each other as "brother" and "sister." Formerly, there were no churches, whereas today, there are 13 evangelical churches there.

On the other hand, a short distance from this town is another town of approximately two thousand or more inhabitants. God's servants have been praying for that town, that satan's principality will be bound, and the mysterious walls of unbelief will be brought down, for there has not been an acceptance of the Gospel or of God's servants. But prayer continues by God's faithful intercessors. Perhaps, you, dear reader, will remember this town in your prayers. We will refer to it as "Town J," using the first letter of the town's name.

Yes, God is doing miracles today, and souls are coming to Jesus.

Jesus said, "I only do the things I see My Father do, and I only say the things I hear My Father say" (see John 5:19). Our Lord moved about from one place to another, as His Father showed Him, but it all had to do with the condition of people's hearts. His Father led Him to the places where His words, confirmed by His miracles, found their way into ready hearts. So it is today.

FAITH

In the area of gifts of power is the gift of *faith*. When I need special help in prayer, I seek someone with faith—someone who not only prays, but prays with conviction, and has the patience to pray it into substance. Those miraculous answers to prayer move our hearts Godward, and stimulate others to do the same. Such persons are, perhaps unknown to them, catalysts, when moved by God's Spirit.

Many years ago, in Africa, there was a pastor who had a mule by which he traveled about to visit the various members of his church. One day, he discovered that his mule had gotten out of his pen and was no place to be found, so he asked several of the brethren to help him search for the mule.

In the meantime, there was a dear widow in her 90's who invited them to her house to pray for the return of the mule. No one showed up. Their anxiety to find the mule was greater than their faith to pray for it. They all went out on the search. Meanwhile, this aged child of faith went to prayer. But she also hung a rope, ready with a slipknot, on her wall, as she continued the day in prayer. Toward late afternoon, she heard some mule-type noises, and turned around to find that the mule had put his head through her window, as if to say, "Here I am." Gently, she removed the rope from the wall next to the window, slipped it over his head, and led the mule to the pastor's house.

The sun was going down, and the group, downhearted, was just returning from their fruitless mission, when the little widow of faith showed up with the pastor's mule tied to her rope! All were amazed, and the pastor asked her why the mule had come to her. Her answer was as simple as her childlike faith—"Because I prayed."

I have said before, Africa was my real school. It took some time for me to reject the Cessation Theology that I had been taught, along with its "lateral damages." God wants us to dare to believe and act on His promises, but above all, to allow Him to search deeply into our hearts to remove the barriers between Him and us. If we do not have the communion with Him that we desire, we know that there are yet some barriers within us to be removed. Not only will these barriers prevent us from enjoying the sweet fellowship with Him, which we both want and need, but they will hinder us from doing the works that Jesus did, along with the function of the spiritual gifts which He has bestowed upon us. If we let a fleshly desire remain within us, that will be all the barrier satan needs to keep us from realizing the plan of God for us and through us.

Faith in general, and faith as a specific gift have much in common. God said to Abraham: "I have made thee a father of many nations" (Rom. 4:17a). Abraham "staggered not at the promise of God through unbelief; but was strong in faith, giving glory to God; and being fully persuaded that what He had promised, He was able also to perform" (Rom. 4:20-21). Abraham had come a long way on the road of faith in his old age. There had been many stumbling stones along the way, and though he faltered a few times, his spiritual sight was getting better, for he had learned to "calleth those things which be not as though they were" (Rom. 4:17b). Only those who see the invisible will do the impossible, for they know that the only things of true value are those that are related to the eternal.

We will see as far as the health of our eyes. If our eyes are healthy, then our whole body will be full of light, God's light. We are the apple of Jesus' eye, and as we live in obedience to His commandments, we will maintain clear vision of all that concerns Him—eternal souls and eternity.

A little sign in the window of an optometrist's office in London says it well: "You can't be optimistic, if you have a misty optic." This is truer in the spiritual realm than in the physical. True faith has good spiritual eyesight, and sees into the invisible. Mountains of impossibilities are considered God's opportunities, and never cause dismay, only maximum joy, as James declares (see James 1:2).

Faith, with its clear spiritual vision, is relentless and unintimidated by the size of the mountains or the quantity of obstacles and hurdles along the way. It calls that which is lacking into existence, and commands that which is threatening, out of existence. It sees strongholds and high walls as challenges, and is grateful to God for the opportunity to once again see His glory in the performance of their downfall. Faith is not a complainer, for it has learned that complaining only short-circuits God's working, and soon clouds divine visions into nothingness. Nor is faith a doubter, for it has prepared itself to quench all the fiery darts of "Hath God said?"

Faith is ready to step out of the boat of human security onto turbulent waters of many unknown dangers, simply because it has heard Jesus say, "Come." Faith has learned the sweet sound of that voice, and is unafraid to always respond, "Here am I, Lord. Send me" (see Isa. 6:8). Faith is no longer hurt or bothered by being called "crazy," having learned that those words aren't accompanied by the sweet voice of Jesus. Faith is not focused on the dangers of that which is difficult, nor on the prospects of that which is possible, but only on Jesus, its author and finisher. Faith knows that by keeping its eyes on Jesus, it moves away from being defined as an abstract noun, into the reality of the substance of the promise, now called a concrete noun.

Faith is not discouraged by those who cannot see into the invisible. Rather it chooses to uphold and encourage them, for it has stumbled along the same path, as a weakling, as also did Father Abraham. It knows that patience will do its perfect work in the end, and is not moved to the right or the left by any of these things. Faith always recalls that God is forever on the throne, and that He is in perfect control of every situation, that nothing takes Him by surprise, that no test is allowed to come our way without His approval first. Faith understands that when trials come, our heavenly Father has already provided the means of bearing up under them and also provided the way of escape from satan's wrath, straight into the arms of our loving Savior who has prepared still greater blessings from His riches in glory (see 1 Cor. 10:13).

Faith, as it grows, pushes anxiety out the door, and says, "Now rest, my child, for I will guard that door. You cannot, but I can, so relax."

Faith's direction is first from God to man, before it reciprocates back to God. Faith, like the newly conceived child, is smaller than a mustard seed, but is ready to grow by the water of God's Word, and the water of God's Spirit, for it comes by "hearing, and hearing by the word of God" (Rom. 10:17b). So then, faith originates with God, not with man, even as man's spirit (the real you) originates with God, not with man. However, it is man who decides what he will feed his spirit, just as he decides what he will feed his body.

Faith, numerically, is seventh in the order of the fruits of the Spirit, which all flow from God: love, joy, peace, longsuffering, gentleness, goodness, faith, meekness, temperance. So faith flows out of God's love. Love is from God, for God is love. Faith, being number seven, is six plus one. Six, man's number, created on the sixth day, plus one—that One, being none other than Jesus, our Lord and Savior. Faith, number seven, is also three plus four—three, the number of God the Trinity, in the third Heaven, plus four, the number of earth (four directions, four seasons, four elements), the combination making faith accessible to us on earth. How we need faith!

Jesus said, "Have faith in God" (Mark 11:22b). But let us look closer at this Scripture. In the original Greek, it says, "Have the faith of God," not "have faith in God." "Have faith in God," means to put your faith in God. The second, "have the faith of God" means to let God's faith be put into you. It means just the opposite. When we have His faith in us, we can reciprocate that faith back to Him.

How do we get His faith into us? The disciples told Jesus, "Lord, increase our faith" (Luke 17:5b). He answered simply by saying, "Have the faith of God." How does it increase? He makes it so clear, but we could easily miss it by looking beyond it. He just says, "Have it!" It is like a mother with a plate of cookies who holds them out to her children, saying, "Have some." Just say, "Thank You, Lord, for another portion of Your faith today," and it is yours! Praise the Lord—it's yours! Indeed, the grateful heart is a receptive heart. What do you need? Reach out for the "cookies of faith." They're especially prepared for you and me.

Chapter Twenty-three

THE LAW OF FAITH VERSUS THE LAW OF GRAVITY

⚓

After our Lord had fed the five thousand in the desert, soon the people began returning to their towns and villages. Knowing already about the fierce wind storm that would strike the Sea of Galilee within a few hours, He constrained His disciples to board their little ship and row over to the other side. Though their hearts would be overtaken by fear, He felt assured of His Father's love and care for them. As the sun descended behind the mountain, He ascended to a solitary place to pray, and there opened His heart to the Father, interceding for them. The evening turned into the black of midnight as He continued in close communion with His Father.

JESUS SAYS, "COME"

It was just past three A.M. when Jesus, perceiving in His spirit the danger His disciples were facing in the middle of the sea, came down from the mountain, and proceeded on foot across the top of the water. The storm tossed their little boat about, filling their hearts with panic, and suddenly they saw "a ghost" walking on the water. This was too much! Perhaps at that moment they were thinking, *Why, oh why, did our Master send us into this?* Then suddenly, Jesus spoke the very words they needed to hear: "Be of good cheer; it is I; be not afraid" (Matt. 14:27b). It doesn't seem that He gave His name to identify Himself; He simply said, "It is I." The tender compassionate voice could not be mistaken, for no ghost would speak like that. It was their Master who had constrained them to get into the boat.

Amidst the fright and confusion of the occasion, many thoughts passed through their minds as they tried to comprehend it all. But that voice! The same voice that lovingly and firmly commanded them into the tiny ship on peaceful waters. While the storm raged and the disciples clung to the boat, Peter was moved by the words of Jesus: "It is I; be not afraid." They were comforting, encouraging words that seemed to challenge his adventurous nature. "Lord, if it be Thou, bid me come unto Thee" (Matt. 14:28b). The Lord had already expected this reaction. "Come," He invited (Matt. 14:29a). The very word was full of authority and security, and caused a bit of faith to come into Peter. And with that tiny faith, Peter stepped out of the boat and began to walk on the water, overcoming the law of gravity which would have normally pulled him under!

Many a sermon has been preached on why Peter sank, but seldom is one heard on why he was able to walk on the water in the first place. Why?

1. Because he wanted to do so.

2. Because Jesus said, "Come."

3. Because that word "Come" inspired enough faith to overcome the law of gravity. Of course, it was God's power that sustained him, but faith had made the connection to receive it.

There is a point at which we must be willing to leave the natural, limited security of our little boat, our family, our friends, and take time to hear that faith-giving word, "Come."

JESUS SAYS, "GO"

We must also hear the word, "Go."

> *Go ye into all the world, and* **preach** *the gospel to every creature...And these signs shall follow them that believe; In My name shall they* **cast out devils***; they shall speak with new tongues; they shall take up serpents; and if they drink any deadly thing, it shall not hurt them; they shall* **lay hands on the sick, and they shall recover** (Mark 16:15b;17-18, emphasis added).

Here we find the threefold ministry that Jesus did: Preaching; Healing the sick; Casting out demons. The faith that overcomes all the obstacles that pull us in the wrong direction is found the moment we respond not only to the "Come," but also to the "Go." Faith means that there will be obedience. Where there is no obedience, there is no faith; and where there is no faith, there is no power; where there is no power, there will be no signs, wonders, or miracles.

"Go" means just that. It leaves no one out. Go across the street. Go across the town. Go across the nation, and go across the ocean. Just go. We can't get around it, nor should we want to.

In the first miracle of our Lord, the water did not turn into wine until it was drawn out. You have been filling yourself with the water of God's Word, and when you begin to draw it out for others, you will see the miracles take place before your eyes. People will then comment that it is the best they ever tasted. Perhaps you have prayed for someone's healing, and you haven't seen any results. Now be brave. Step out of the boat. Lay on hands, thank God for the healing He has provided, and command the sickness out in the name of Jesus. Get ready for surprises! He will fulfill, if we will only obey. Then let Him be glorified for what He does.

JESUS SAYS, "HAVE FAITH"

Faith comes from Him, power comes from Him, and healing comes from Him. So now, the glory must go to Him. There will be no more receiving of power without the giving of praise. He who gives shall also receive—another law. Give unto the Lord, and He shall give back unto you, many times over (see Luke 6:38). When you receive from Him, whether faith, love, power, or authority, give back the praise to Him who sitteth upon the throne. If you neglect to do so, the cycle will stop, and we should not wonder why.

The apostles one day told the Lord, "Increase our faith" (Luke 17:5b). This is surely the kind of request that God likes to hear, and notice how He responded to it. Instead of lining them up and laying His hands on them to receive more faith, He said,

> *If ye had faith as a grain of mustard seed, ye might say unto this sycamine tree, Be thou plucked up by the root, and be thou planted in the sea; and it should obey you* (Luke 17:6).

He did not increase their faith, but rather gave *them* the key to increasing it.

We all would love an increase in faith, but it is not acquired quickly by the waving of a wand. Rather, He challenged them to begin to use the tiny amount of faith they had to tackle a difficult problem—the uprooting of the tough, deep-rooted sycamine tree, and casting it into the sea. Notice that He did not say that we should pray to ask the Father to uproot it, but that we should speak to it with our own tongue. This is not a prayer, much less a mind prayer. Likewise, He commands *us* to *command the tree:* "Be thou plucked up by the root, and be thou planted in the sea." And then He assures us: "And it should obey you."

The problems in life may seem to us like the law of gravity. Your weight, for instance, is determined not only by what you eat, but also by the size of the earth. So, if the earth were smaller, you would weigh less. But it matters not what size the earth is, nor what size your problem is, the law of faith can counteract and overcome it.

Peter might have weighed 200 pounds, but when Jesus said, "Come," he stepped out of the boat, believing in the very One who said that word. And it worked! At least for a few steps, it worked perfectly. But what went wrong? The boisterous wind and waves made him fearful, and he doubted whether or not he could continue. Likewise, have you started off well? Has something gone wrong? Listen to the very words that Jesus said to him: "O thou of little faith, wherefore didst thou doubt?" (Matt. 14:31b).

Fear came in, and doubts along with it. His faith then shrank to less than the mustard seed. This is where we need to pay close attention. There will always be things in this life that may intimidate and make us fearful. Then come the doubts (faith shrinkers). It is important to daily be "Looking unto Jesus [not the problem] the author and finisher of our faith" (Heb. 12:2a); then we will be able to run the race with patience.

Let us be ready for any type of problem in this life. If not, we will surely go under. So, how do we get ready?

1. Always look steadfastly to Jesus;
2. Keep listening to His tender voice; and
3. Step out of the boat. It is better than clinging to it.

The Christian life is the Christ-life. "To live is Christ" (Phil. 1:21). It is a life of miracles, impossibilities becoming realities, hate becoming love, sadness and depression becoming abundant joy.

There are some who are reading these lines who, for years, have struggled with a deep-rooted sycamine tree of depression. You cannot counsel this tree out of the ground. It will not budge. Jesus has already given you the exact words to use on such a rooted problem: "Be plucked up by the root, and be thou planted in the sea." The faith that is the size of a mustard seed will do it. This faith is just big enough to be able to say, "I'll do it!" Then it does. And when it does, that mustard seed of faith increases to many times its size. How? When you see that tree obey you, as Jesus said it would, your faith has only one way to go.

Chapter Twenty-four

GET READY FOR
WHAT IS COMING

⚓

The clock cannot be turned back. The "good ole days" are gone. But much better ones are ahead, for He has said, "I will pour out My spirit upon all flesh," and "Lo, I am with you always, even unto the end of the world" (Joel 2:28; Matt: 28:20).

But now the Spirit of God is speaking expressly in these latter days:

> *This know also, that in the last days perilous times shall come. For men shall be lovers of their own selves, covetous, boasters, proud, blasphemers, disobedient to parents, unthankful, unholy, without natural affection, trucebreakers, false accusers, incontinent, fierce, despisers of those that are good, traitors, heady, highminded, lovers of pleasures more than lovers of God; having a form of godliness, but denying the power thereof...(2 Timothy 3:1-5).*

Our Lord has told us, "As the days of Noah were, so shall also the coming of the Son of Man be" (Matt. 24:37). In Genesis 6:11, we find that just prior to the flood, the whole earth was filled with corruption and violence. Today, once again, the whole earth is filled with corruption and violence. The love of pleasure rather than the love of God has brought sleep to entire nations while the time bomb of Islamic violence has crept into Europe. In addition, a quiet preparation of terrorist activities is under way in the United States. God's archenemy, satan, is moving under the guise of religion with that ever insatiable desire to be worshipped. He knows that his time is short, and he is preparing his man, into whose flesh he will step, in order to be worshipped. Paul says that he will go into the temple and present himself as God (see 2 Thess. 2:3-4). It then will no longer be enough for him to see only the masses of people around the world bowing down to him, but he will also want the people of Israel to bow down in worship to him in the temple itself. This is his agenda. Daily happenings around the world are lining things up for this grand long-awaited event.

REMOVING THE SPOTS AND WRINKLES

Our Lord is looking for laborers for His harvest, but few are willing to pay the price. His eyes are circling the earth to find one "whose heart is perfect toward Him," through whom He can do mighty things (see 2 Chron. 16:9). A "perfect heart" means one who has surrendered himself 100 percent to the Lord who has bought him.

Paul the apostle says by the Holy Spirit that Christ "loved the church, and gave Himself for it; that He might sanctify and cleanse it with the washing of water by the word, that He might present it to Himself a glorious church, not having spot, or wrinkle, or any such thing; but that it should be holy and without blemish" (Eph. 5:25b-27).

The Church, the Body of believers, is today not without spot or wrinkle. We are told here already that the water of the Word will remove the spots. But what about the wrinkles? It takes a hot iron to remove them. And that iron is coming soon. This will not be the heat of the Great Tribulation. Rather, there is coming upon us now what is called "the beginning of sorrows," which is the beginning of "labor pains" (see Matt. 24:8; Mark 13:8). As time goes on, they will occur closer and closer together. Yet it all takes place before the removal of the Church, which is still quite wrinkled. The times will become so difficult that many Christians will believe they are in the Great Tribulation. These times will be sufficient to remove the wrinkles, nothing more, for God has not appointed us to that phase of His wrath, which is to come in the "time of Jacob's trouble" (Jer. 30:7).

Along with destruction, violence, and persecution, we will also soon see a time of sweet refreshing and of great revival, sweeping through one place after another. There are sparks of this today. The flame of God's holiness, which burned in the bush before Moses, will burn again, without stopping until the Church goes up. Then among the chaos and confusion resulting from the disappearance of the Church, the super power, which is the United States, will be unable to protect Israel. Islamic countries, growing by the day, will become extremely powerful. Israel, then with most of her people having returned to the land, will feel hopeless, surrounded by those who hate her.

A FALSE LEADER VERSUS GOD'S WITNESSES

In the meantime, a "little horn" of mysterious authority will rise. He will talk about love and peace, and will have the charm of one who has been transformed into an angel of light. He has been in Eden (see Ezek. 28). Indeed, the first beast and the last beast are the same beast. He will have a golden tongue and a convincing smile, and could well be of Jewish blood, for the Jews will be willing to listen to him. But at the same time, he could be of the Islamic religion, for Muslims will also be willing to listen to him.

Whatever the case, he persuades the followers of Mohammed to give up the Dome of the Rock, proposing an agreement for the immediate construction of the temple, for he will say, "Are we not all the children of Abraham?" They will have heard it before, again, and again, and again. But now, for some reason, it seems like a good idea. With chaos throughout the world, people will be looking for a new, powerful leader, for they will be ready for a one-world government. This man will seemingly have all the answers, and will speak to them with authority. He will be slick, not unlike the serpent, even down to the forked tongue, which will enable him to speak the way that both sides want to hear. He will be able to put it all together, for his time has come.

Things will look rosy for Israel…for a while. They will be thrilled at the prospect of watching their beloved temple go up so quickly. Surely this must be their Messiah. And things will look rosy for satan, as he watches the progress of the temple, where soon he will be worshipped, and will bask in the light of being a world leader, enjoying the applause and standing ovations. His base of operation will be in Babylonia (modern day Iraq), which will become the glory of the world, due to its riches and its position.

Meanwhile, God will never be without a witness—144,000 of them (12,000 from each of the 12 tribes), and the two Old Testament witnesses (Elijah, and probably Moses). A great revival will get underway, and millions of people will "wash their garments in the blood of the Lamb" (see Rev. 7:13-17), "a great multitude, which no man could number" (Rev. 7:9a). The persecution and suffering will be much greater than before the departure of the Church, and the spiritual fruit of the revival will be greater, as well.

He Is Ready to Do His Works Through You

Now, getting back to us today. Our Father is ready to pour out His Spirit on His children now! Listen to His words: "Turn you at My reproof: behold I will pour out My Spirit unto you, I will make known My words unto you" (Prov. 1:23). We should not need more violence and terrorism to bring us to our senses. We may indeed hear His voice now, saying, "Come, step out of the boat. Follow Me, and I will make you fishers of men." It is safe to walk with Him. Indeed, it is blessed! It is transforming to look into the face of our Savior. Truly, it is faith-giving and life-changing.

Never mind the group of friends who cling to natural security, where the boat is rocking and the knees are knocking. Never mind the height of the waves, nor the roar of the wind. Jesus is there. He is on top of it all, and in control of it all. Gravity does not affect Him—He made it, too. He is just a call away. His hand will lift you, should you doubt.

Afraid to step out of the boat? His perfect love will cast out that fear, and He says to you now, "Call unto Me, and I will answer thee, and show thee great and mighty things, which thou knowest not" (Jer. 33:3). He is ready to do His works through you. His signs and wonders have not ceased. What has ceased is faith on our part, for we should keep before us that "these signs shall follow them that believe" (Mark 16:17a). Jesus said to Thomas, "Reach hither thy hand, and thrust it into My side: and be not faithless, but believing" (John 20:27b).

Faith stops when we say, "I will not believe it unless I see it." This is where the "cessation" part comes in. When faith ceases, miracles cease. Thomas, glory to God, ceased being an unbelieving believer. When he saw the Savior and looked upon those wounds, he knew that this was truly his resurrected Lord, and the power of that resurrection became his, through faith. But faith that is born within, without seeing is faith that is blessed. For Jesus said, "Thomas, because thou hast seen Me, thou hast believed: *blessed* are they that have not seen, and yet have believed" (John 20:29, emphasis added).

Beloved reader, you have heard these words of Jesus, and you have read the testimonies of what He has been doing. Do you also need to see with your eyes? Step out of the boat. He says, "Come." There are many blessings awaiting you, and all around you today are events taking place that satan is using to make hearts fearful. Remember these comforting words of our Lord: "Let not your heart be troubled, neither let it be afraid" (John 14:27b).

The very events of today, as evil as they are, will provide the opportunities that we need to become the instruments of God's grace to people all around the world. The fields are white unto harvest, and the laborers are few. Let us pray that the Lord of the harvest will send forth laborers where He has prepared the hearts and the circumstances to reap the many souls who are ready to come to Him. Jesus is coming soon. Let us be occupied in His will.

Chapter Twenty-five
STEP OUT OF THE BOAT

⚓

Dear friend, before we part, I would like to share a few more thoughts from my heart. I pray that you have been blessed by reading these testimonies of what Jesus has done and will do through you, if you will let Him. I also pray that you remember Him, not us. As Paul the apostle says, "Your life is hid with Christ in God" (Col. 3:3b). To live is Christ, not Levi, nor Lily, and to die is gain (see Phil. 1:21). To die physically is to gain Jesus and our heavenly home. In the meantime, to die to self is to gain His presence with us on earth right now. He can then walk in these shoes, and talk with this mouth. He can express His love through us, as He did when He walked this earth. Are you ready for that?

FIRST DEATH, THEN RESURRECTION

To be honest, I still find a large gap between what I am and what I should be. I find that there are areas still within me that He wants to change. So I must continue to pray, as David did,

"Search me, O God, and know my heart: try me, and know my thoughts: and see if there be any wicked way in me, and lead me in the way everlasting" (Ps. 139: 23-24). God has given us a makeup like His own, in His image and likeness. There is room for the total person and character of Jesus within us. But there is need for us to not only die once and for all to self, but also, as Paul says, to "die daily," as the Holy Spirit reveals to us the areas of our lives that we have not yet surrendered to the Lord. We need to let Him search us, because often we ourselves are ignorant of our own weaknesses and rebellions within.

Jesus said, "If any man will come after Me, let him deny himself, and take up his cross daily, and follow Me" (Luke 9:23). It is now *our* cross, not His, and it is death to self on a daily basis. This requires a decision, and it requires effort, but the power to perform comes from Him. There is resurrection power for you and for me, but there cannot be a resurrection until there is a death.

Yes, Jesus will do all the works through you that He did while walking this earth, and more. However, self must be emptied out. Let's allow Him to speak to us about those things that must go. He has paid a great price for you and for me. Do we truly understand just how much it cost Him? When we allow the Holy Spirit to reveal these things to us, we will never be the same again. Let us invite Him to begin that search, and to work that transformation, which we need in order for Jesus to live His life within us, and to do His wonders through us. It is a wonderful, joyful life. It is a life with the daily presence of Jesus, which brings His praises continually to our lips, like a spring that never ceases to flow.

THE GREATEST OF THESE IS LOVE

There is great joy in serving Jesus. The greatest joy of all flows out of the love of Jesus, for "the fruit of the Spirit is love, joy, peace, longsuffering, gentleness, goodness, faith, meekness, temperance" (Gal. 5: 22-23). "The fruit of the Spirit is love," and the other eight fruits flow out of love. Love is the very essence of God's character. When love increases to the point of overflowing, it becomes joy. Peace follows. But love, the love of God, is what we need the most. Only love has four dimensions. Everything else on this earth that can be measured has just three dimensions—length, width, and height. All these things are finite and temporal.

On the other hand, if you go outside at night and look up at the stars, try to imagine a wall on the other side of those stars. Of course, there is none. But if there were, what would be on the other side of that wall? You see, when you look away from this earth, and into God's heavens, you are seeing into four dimensions, because that fourth dimension brings it into infinity.

Now look into the Word of God, to the place, the only place, where you find the mention of four dimensions. It is found in Ephesians 3:14-21. This was the prayer of the apostle Paul, by the Holy Spirit:

> *That ye…may be able to comprehend with all saints what is the* **breadth**, *and* **length**, *and* **depth**, *and* **height**; *and to know the love of Christ, which passeth knowledge, that ye might be filled with all the fullness of God* (Ephesians 3:18-19, emphasis added).

Do you want the fullness of God in your life? Then you need the fullness of His love, for God is love. It is the essence of His character.

THE VALUE OF SOULS

When we receive the nature of Christ within us, then He can love others through us. The harvest of souls is very great today, but the laborers are few. We are praying that the Lord of the harvest will send forth laborers into His harvest.

In most places of Latin America today, one can go to the parks and plazas and find souls who are hungry for God. In a few hours of one day, several of them can be brought to Jesus, just by one person, one at a time. The Holy Spirit is moving in hearts everywhere, for the coming of our Lord is drawing nigh. They need to sense the love of God in the message we bring to them.

Jesus said in His prayer to His Father (see John 17) something that needs to sink profoundly into our hearts. Seven times over, He referred to us as "those whom Thou hast given Me." This is found in verses 2, 6, 9, 11, 12, and 24. You may ask, "Why is this significant?" The reason is because *we* are the *Father's gift* to the Son. Does this help us to see the value that the Father places on us? Is it not reasonable that He would want to give Him that which His heart desired the most? And what do we do about gathering these gifts for Him? They are the souls who are all around us, the ones who are waiting to come to Jesus. They are everywhere. But if we are not in communion with our Lord, we will miss them. If we are bothered by anxiety in our lives, we will not notice them. If material things are important to us, the souls who God loves will not be important to us.

> *For God, who commanded the light to shine out of darkness, hath shined in our hearts, to give the light of the knowledge of the glory of God in the face of Jesus Christ. But we have this treasure in earthen vessels, that the excellency of the power may be of God, and not of us* (2 Corinthians 4:6-7).

This is our opportunity, and what a glorious one it is! We have the excellency of the power, yes, right now, in these earthen vessels, these clay pots, to bring many souls to Jesus! The time is short. Every day that passes is another day closer to the coming of our Lord, another day closer to eternity! How many souls have we missed today while we spent our time on temporal affairs? "They that be wise shall shine as the brightness of the firmament; and they that turn many to righteousness as the stars for ever and ever" (Dan. 12:3).

We need the Holy Spirit to not only break and mold our spirits, but also to remove the scales from our eyes, so that we can see things as God sees them, that we might move from the realm of the temporal into the realm of the eternal. "While we look not at the things which are seen, but at the things which are not seen: for the things which are seen are temporal; but the things which are not seen are eternal" (2 Cor. 4:18).

SEE HIS GLORY AND DO GREATER WORKS

"Looking at the things which are not seen…" Is this possible? To see things which are not seen? With God, all things are possible. Martha, sister of Lazarus who died, said to Jesus, "Lord, by this time he stinketh: for he hath been dead four days" (John 11:39b). Jesus had waited those days so that Lazarus *would* die, and so He does with us. He is waiting for us to die to self, to the point of stinking, so that He can use us for His glory. Jesus answered Martha, "Said I not unto thee, that if thou wouldest believe, thou shouldest see the glory of God?" (John 11:40).

God is ready to show His glory through you. Are you ready to die to self? Die, and He will remove the stench, and do many things for His glory through you. Yet if we begin to desire any glory for ourselves, then we must again go through death and the stench.

Let us remember the inspired words of the apostle Paul,

> *I am crucified with Christ: nevertheless I live; yet not I, but Christ liveth in me: and the life which I now live in the flesh I live by the faith of the Son of God, who loved me, and gave Himself for me* (Galatians 2:20).

We are to be crucified with Him, that is, dead to self, though our bodies live on. It is now Christ that lives and moves within us, to walk in our shoes, to talk with our mouths, to heal with our hands. You and I can't do it, but He can! Are you ready to turn it all over to Him? He is ready to do it. "Faithful is He that calleth you, who also will do it" (1 Thess. 5:24). He has said that He would do even greater works through us than He did then, because He goes to His Father (see John 14:12). Now read this verse about doing greater works, and then connect it to the following verse because they are joined by the word "and." "And whatsoever ye shall ask in My name, that will I do, that the Father may be glorified in the Son" (John 14:13). Apparently, the greater works are connected to *asking*, so that the Father may be glorified in the Son. Then He repeats His promise because it is so important, "If ye shall ask any thing in My name, I will do it" (John 14:14). What a powerful promise this is! We lack nothing. He provides everything. However, we must be willing to leave the security of our little boat. By trying to save our own life, we may lose it. Jesus gave His life to save ours. "Greater love hath no man than this, that a man lay down his life for his friends" (John 15:13).

The night is coming when no man can work. It is time to bring in the harvest. It will be a huge harvest, and there will be both tears and rejoicing. "They that sow in tears shall reap in joy. He that goeth forth and weepeth, bearing precious seed, shall doubtless come again with rejoicing, bringing his sheaves with him" (Ps. 126:5-6).

While the harvest is great, the laborers are few. Isaiah says, "I heard the voice of the Lord, saying, Whom shall I send, and who will go for Us? Then said I, Here am I; send me" (Isa. 6:8).

Will you go? Will you pray?

CONTACT THE AUTHOR

If you would like to receive our newsletter via e-mail
and pray for the needs in the harvest fields,
please contact us via e-mail at the address listed below.
We look forward to hearing from you.

Levi_and_Lily@hotmail.com

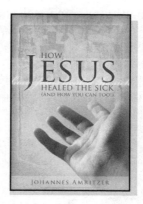